A New English Primer

AN INTRODUCTION TO
LINGUISTIC CONCEPTS
AND SYSTEMS

William R. Elkins

KANSAS STATE
TEACHERS COLLEGE

MACMILLAN

For Steve, Sue, and Bill

Preface

Lately there has been a surge of interest in the information provided by contemporary linguistic research, and teachers of English increasingly are encouraged, if not required, to include some elements of linguistics in both secondary-school and elementary-school curricula or to use linguistically oriented language arts textbooks in their classrooms. All of this interest in linguistics is good, but my experience as an instructor of both prospective and practicing teachers has led me to believe that new linguistic information is too often lost to them simply because they lack a grasp of fundamental linguistic concepts. That is the problem to which this book is addressed.

Perhaps I should say here what the book is *not*: it is not an attempt to extend the frontiers of linguistic inquiry or even, for that matter, to report much of what is happening on those frontiers, although that is both important and fascinating. Rather, the book—as its title implies—is an attempt to present the concepts that are useful to a basic understanding and appreciation of contemporary linguistic systems. It differs from other textbooks in that it introduces only the most important concepts, leaving to the student (or the instructor) the decision to pursue any or all of them further. It relates these concepts to both structural and generative-transformational grammars, providing a background that should help students to adapt to the variations in terminology and method that they will encounter in their later reading. The book also draws explicit parallels between structural and generative-transformational grammars and, where appropriate, discusses the strengths and weaknesses of the different modes of inquiry.

Each chapter concludes with a brief list of readings, meant as a guide to more extended explanations than a primer such as this one permits. In addition, a selected bibliography can be found in Appendix C. At intervals in the text there are exercises for the student to try if he wishes, and in Appendix A there are suggested applications of the book's concepts. Neither the exercises nor the applications are intended to be prescriptive: ideally the study of language should be a creative activity, one in which students choose their own areas of concentration.

The selected bibliography, suggested readings, and notes acknowledge my debt to those scholars whose works influenced this book. I owe much to the many students who responded to various drafts of the book, and I am grateful for valuable commentary from many reviewers, especially my colleague Melvin G. Storm. Charles E. Walton, another colleague and chairman of my department, gave tangible form to his encouragement by arranging for clerical assistance and a convenient class schedule. My thanks go also to the staff of St. Martin's Press for their patience, concern, and editorial expertise in bringing this book into print.

William R. Elkins

Contents

ONE

Language and English Linguistics

How do we who speak the same language understand each other? Some undoubtedly will say that we communicate because we know the same sounds. Some may say that we communicate because we know the same words. And some may say that we communicate because we make words from the sounds and place those words in a certain order. Only those who give the last answer approach the truth of the matter.

Language is made up of sounds; sounds make units that in many languages are considered *words;* words pattern into units that in many languages are considered *sentences.* However, if we stop at this point—and most of us do because we give little more thought to our use of language than to the act of walking—we ignore the fact that language is potentially as scientifically describable as are the parts of the body that permit us to walk. As biology is the science that uncovers the interaction of bone, tendon, and muscle in bodily movement, *linguistics* is the science that uncovers the fundamentals of the systematic hierarchy of human communication: (1) sound; (2) meaning-bearing unit (for now we'll call it a *word*); and (3) structural unit (for now we'll call it a *sentence*). The analogy can be expanded: biology is the science of living organisms because it investigates and describes these organisms; linguistics is the science of language because it investigates and describes languages.

For some four decades American linguists have developed concepts of the English language which to varying degrees apply to languages in general. Our purpose here will be to examine the pertinent concepts and use them to develop systems and schematic representations that will assist us in comprehending the basic simplicity yet infinite complexity of English.

A Definition of Language

Language may be defined as a system of vocal symbols that provides human beings with the means to communicate. The system and the kind of vocality are to a degree arbitrarily determined by each group of speakers. When two sets of systematic vocal symbols are so different that their users cannot communicate, two languages exist: "Avez-vous étudié le français?" and "Have you studied French?" ask the same question, but they ask it so differently that each represents a segment of a distinct, unique language.

On the other hand, vocal and structural features may differ significantly yet still retain enough similarity for people to communicate. For instance, "You all come to my party" and "Yawl come tuh muh pahty" convey the same message to all speakers of English. Similarly, though "Throw Mama from the Train a Kiss"—the title of a once-popular song—is a distortion of standard English structural order, English speakers can sort out the intended message. In traveling around the United States, Americans often hear different words used for the same thing: the terms *flapjack, hotcake, pancake,* and *griddlecake* are peculiar to regions and social levels, but the chances are that a person will understand whatever version he encounters. While the statement "I need some bread" can refer to either loaves or money, the context will usually make the meaning clear. When differences such as these are present, we do not have two languages, or three, or however many; we have *dialects* of the same language. Often the exact line between *dialect* and *language* is difficult to draw, but generally linguists agree that regional influences combined with ethnic, age, social, professional, and educational differences contribute to dialect distinctions.

We can now enlarge on some fundamental aspects of language:

1. Each language is *unique*. Historical and comparative linguistics reveal family relationships among languages, but the uniqueness of each language calls for an independent description. Traditional or "school" grammar, which has dominated the teaching of English since the eighteenth century, attempts to apply to English the grammatical terms, rules, and concepts of Latin. While such an attempt may be partially successful, its overall influence must inevitably lead to misconceptions about the precise nature of the English language.

2. Language is *system*. A language must have form and order if it is to be functional.

3. Language is *vocal*. Any attempt to disregard the primary vocality of language overlooks the way we ourselves acquire language and ignores what even a cursory understanding of the history of man tells us about the advent of writing. All of us made good use of our ability to communicate vocally for a number of years before we learned to write. And written language has existed figuratively but a second or so in proportion to the time man has existed. Many languages exist today without a written form, and many undoubtedly existed and "died" without ever acquiring a written form. Moreover, written language can hardly account for those features that we express with gesture, intonation, and other such qualities that make our utterances uniquely our own. Linguists are giving increasing attention to *kinesics,* so-called body language; *proxemics,* the way in which speakers use distance; and *paralanguage* features, the intonational qualities by which speakers express emotions and attitudes.

4. Language is *symbolic*. Among all animals man, as far as we know, has the most highly developed ability to symbolize. Indeed, many profound thinkers believe that it is man's ability to symbolize that sets him apart from other members of the animal world. In addition, man can create symbol systems based on other symbol systems. Writing is, of course, one symbolic representation of language; others such as Morse code, pictographs, and sign language come quickly to mind.

5. Language is *arbitrary*. It is true that some obvious external forces, forming a part of our perception of reality, help to limit and determine whatever language we use. We live

in a world of "things" and "actions" which we want to express symbolically. Languages will generally have noun forms for the "things" and verb forms for the "actions." We need to represent time; languages generally reflect this need. We need to ask questions and give orders; languages generally reflect these needs as well. But beyond the obvious external limitations, systems and vocality are highly arbitrary.

An English speaker, for example, may create a question from the statement *you like to swim* by inverting the word order and adding the form *do;* that is, he may say *do you like to swim?* A Thai speaker may say cʰɔɔp|wǎy|nám|máy (represented in a linguist's notation); this translates literally to *like swim water question particle.* An English speaker may say *he ate his food with him,* but a Thai speaker represents simple past time contextually, shows possession differently, and does not bother with case; thus kʰáw | tʰaan | ahǎan | kʰɔɔŋ | kʰáw | káp | kʰáw translates to *he eat food of he with he.* Thai and its related Sino-Tibetan languages also choose to use intonational features, mainly pitch, to distinguish meaning: /kʰǎw/ means *mountain:* /kʰǎaw/ with a long vowel means *white.* Japanese, which is not Sino-Tibetan, also shows arbitrary features. An English speaker wanting to utter *he can see* can use only those word forms and in the order noted. A Japanese speaker may choose either [kare wa miru kotoga dekiru], which translates to *he subject position see can,* or [kare wa mirareru], which also translates to *he subject position see can.*[1]

These examples show how different languages arbitrarily represent the same things in different ways. A related point can be made concerning recent studies of human instinct. Although many contemporary linguists and psychologists now believe that human beings possess an instinctive drive to acquire language, this belief does not imply that instinct determines the particular forms of a language. There is no reason to suppose that a new-born child in Thailand or Japan has an instinct for Thai or Japanese grammar as opposed to English grammar. In this sense, too, language is arbitrary.

6. Language permits *human communication.* This is obviously the basic function of language. But it is not easy to determine the exact relationship between the "thoughts" we communicate and the language we use to embody them. For

instance, can a person think without language? Are, in fact, language and thought simultaneous? These questions, not yet completely answered, are part of the concern of those who work in *psycholinguistics,* the psychology of language.

At this point we should identify a distinction that is important to recent linguistic research. This distinction between *competence* and *performance* represents the difference between what a speaker knows about his language—the *competence* that allows him to create and understand an infinite number of utterances because he has learned his language's underlying system—and how a speaker uses his language—his *performance* in producing actual utterances. Naturally, competence and performance interact constantly by allowing a speaker-listener to communicate and comprehend as he accepts, questions, or rejects linguistic performance. For instance, a speaker may utter, *well it's like no that's not right it's like one of those things that goes [appropriate gesture] you know* . . . . It is possible that *[appropriate gesture] you know* communicates, but it is likely that the listener will say, "No, I don't understand" or "What do you mean?" because the speaker's fragmented performance has not fulfilled the listener's sense of competence.

It is possible to identify two dominant directions of modern linguistic research related to the competence-performance distinction: *structuralism,* which relies primarily on the description of utterances (performance) as a means to develop formal descriptive systems, and *generative-transformationalism,* which attempts to describe not utterances as such but rather the underlying system (competence) as a model of the way the speaker-listener creates and comprehends utterances. But just as we cannot separate competence and performance, a description of an underlying system cannot succeed unless it validates its assumptions to some degree by the utterances in the language under study. This does not mean that structuralism and generative-transformationalism are compatible or that one set of theories may be described in terms of the other. It does mean that modern linguistic research can be better comprehended and its theories, both existing and yet to be proposed, more lucidly presented when correspondences are drawn.

Grammar

The term *grammar* is perhaps one of the most misused and misunderstood words that pertain to language. Generally, the term has come to encompass not only the structure of a language but also aspects of usage and social acceptability.

To define "grammar" correctly, we should go back to the three elements we mentioned in connection with the analogy between biology and linguistics: sound, meaning-bearing unit, and structural unit. Translating these into a more formal terminology, we can say that the grammar of a language consists of the *phonology*, the *morphology*, and the *syntax* of that language. This definition is, for the most part, compatible with the two linguistic systems under consideration in this text. Noam Chomsky, whose theoretical works provide the basis for generative-transformational grammars, contends that a grammar is the sentences of a language; these sentences have a phonological component, a syntactic component, and a semantic component which, taken together, provide a grammatical model based on the speaker-hearer's *competence*.[2] In contrast, a model statement for a structural grammar attempts to categorize significant *performance* features in the areas of phonology, morphology, and syntax. At this point, we will define the latter three terms in the context of structural grammars and in Chapter Two we will relate them to structural systems. In Chapter Three, we will expand our understanding of Chomsky's terms and relate them to generative-transformational grammars.

PHONOLOGY

Phonology is a term that encompasses the vocal features of language. Phonology is generally divided into two major areas of study: *phonetics* and *phonemics*.

Phonetics is the study of the production, reception, and perception of sound. It has two major branches: *acoustic phonetics* and *articulatory phonetics*. Acoustic phonetics is a descriptive technique that uses electronic devices to investigate the production and perception of sound. Because acoustic phonetic study requires sophisticated equipment and a laboratory environment, it is beyond the scope of this book.

Articulatory phonetic study, on the other hand, deals with

the physiological apparatus in human beings which produces and receives sound. Those engaged in this study have developed a system for transcribing the physiologically produced sounds into a written form that functions for all languages. *The International Phonetic Alphabet* (IPA) prepared by the International Phonetic Association offers symbol forms called *phones* which permit a speaker who knows the IPA to pronounce a word in any language with some degree of accuracy even though he may have no idea what the word means.

A language phenomenon that took place at the end of the fifteenth and beginning of the sixteenth centuries illustrates certain characteristics of articulatory phonetic study. This phenomenon, termed "The Great Vowel Shift," had the effect of shifting the front and back long vowel sounds in English, thus separating English from its related languages on the European continent by giving it a more "close-mouthed" sound. Consider the following diagram.

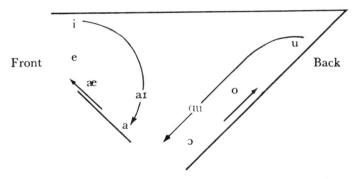

This diagram shows the front and back long vowels affected by the shift. By raising these vowels, causing the tongue to elevate and the oral aperture to decrease in size, English speakers moved from the articulating position represented by the phone symbol [a] to the position represented by the symbol [e]. The word *name* formed by Middle English speakers was phonetically [namə] (rhymes with *mama*), but as formed by Modern English speakers it is phonetically [nem]. The top long vowels broke over into diphthongs; thus Middle English *five* was [fif] (rhymes with *leaf*) but is now [faɪv]. The Middle English top long vowel [u] became the diphthong [ɑu] illustrated by the word *down,* which in Middle English was pro-

nounced [dʌn] (rhymes with *noon*) but is now pronounced
[dɑun]. The above explanation is, of course, only a brief ap-
proximation of what happened; it serves here to identify some
of the workings of articulatory phonetic study and to emphasize that the phone indicates an approximate forming position
in the production of human speech sounds.

Phonemics is the study of the sound features of a given language. Since each language is unique, each will have a unique
sound system. In contrast to articulatory phonetics, which uses
the phone symbol to identify the approximate formation of a
sound regardless of the language, phonemics uses the *phoneme*
—the idea of a sound as distinct from an actual sound—to
identify a class of sounds which are phonetically similar and
which, in context with other characteristics of the language,
distinguish meaning for its speakers. We can initially think of
it this way: say to an English speaker the words *got, grab,
gander, girl, glide* and ask him to state the letter sound that
begins each word. He will undoubtedly say *g;* but if we pronounce each of the above words and give attention to the
articulating process, we readily note that each *g* sound is
phonetically distinct. The *g* in English is actually a variety of
sounds which we conceive of as being the same. The *g* therefore is a phoneme; its different phonetic variations are called
allophones. The allophone is phonetically describable, but the
phoneme, strictly speaking, is not. The logical question, then,
is how linguists determine the phonemes of a given language.

Linguists use several approaches to determine phonemes.
Since the phoneme is an abstraction, they generally use contrasts as part of the identifying technique. The theory or approach that seems best suited to our needs is termed *minimal
pairs.* English words such as *crease* and *grease* are phonetically similar with one exception. The sound /k/ of *crease* and
the sound /g/ of *grease* represent the exception and, at the
same time, establish different meanings for the two words.
These two distinctions, a single difference in sound and a difference in meaning, establish a *minimal pair* and identify
/k/ and /g/ as two English phonemes. The search for minimal pairs continues until the linguist has identified all the
phonemes in the language. Some other examples in English
are *pat* and *pal* which identify /t/ and /l/, *god* and *good*
which identify /a/ and /u/, and so on.[3] The exact number of
English *segmental* phonemes—those that linguists discover by

an approach such as minimal pairs *and* symbolically represent like the examples above—is still open to discussion. We
may say that the various interpretations indicate a number
between thirty-three and thirty-eight. The phonemic branch
also embraces the study of *suprasegmental* phonemes, sound
features that are intonational and act over or above segmental
phonemes to vary and change meaning. As a person speaks,
his voice places emphasis, rises and falls, and pauses. Each
of these variations in intonation in some way modifies or
changes the message. Linguists generally identify three kinds
of suprasegmental phonemes: *stress, pitch,* and *juncture.*
Some linguists have found it effective to identify four kinds of
stress, four levels of pitch, and four kinds of juncture. Such
a classification is, of course, purely an abstraction, as is any
notion that stress, pitch, and juncture work independently of
each other. But we should isolate some contrasts, like those we
examined for segmental phonemes, that emphasize the importance of intonation on linguistic performance.

The term *suspect* shows the importance of stress by forming
two words that are not only distinct in meaning but fill different positions in an utterance. Consider the following:

> The súspect was apprehended by the police.
>
> I suspéct that Joe was wrong.

The effect of *pitch* is evident in the following pair:

> George was here.
> George, come here.

In the first example, *George* may be said with a relatively
normal pitch level, but in the second *George* requires an
elevated pitch and, of course, added stress because the speaker
is uttering an imperative, a call signal.

Juncture, a pause of some duration, may, at one level, determine word boundaries; at another level it may determine
utterance boundaries. The levels, in either case, are not clearly
defined. We can show that juncture is phonemic by noting the
effect on meaning when juncture is moved:

> The gray train of Henry VIII is worth noting.
> The great reign of Henry VIII is worth noting.

These two utterances are identical except for the placement
of the juncture in the pairs of words *gray train* and *great*

reign. Either pair segmentally is /greytreyn/. When the juncture appears between the /y/ and the /t/, the words are *gray
train;* when the juncture appears between the /t/ and the /r/,
the words are *great reign.*

Simply because the distinctions in kinds and levels are so
imprecise, many linguists have adopted a generalized notation
for designating suprasegmental overlays. This notation postu-
lates an *intonation pattern* (IP) that approximates the combined action of stress, pitch, and terminal (end-of-sentence)
juncture. An IP system uses the numbers 1, 2, and 3 to indicate, respectively, low pitch, weak stress, falling terminal contour; medium pitch, normal stress; and higher pitch, heavier
stress, rising terminal contour. It is then possible to identify
three representative intonation patterns:

2-3-1:   George was here.

2-3-3:   Was George here?

3-2-1:   George, come here.

Naturally, speakers vary the patterns. The first utterance need
not be inverted to create a question: use of the 2-3-3 IP, without any change in word order, creates the question *George
was here?*. Similarly, the imperative of the last utterance can
be intensified by using a 3-2-3 IP. Despite these variations, an
IP system appears more workable than does a system that
notes each level of each kind of suprasegmental. We should,
of course, place the dominant stress in the last statement on
workable, because the research linguist must continue to work
toward greater precision. In fact, recent research proposes a
generative phonology, a descriptive model consistent with the
theoretical basis of generative-transformational grammars.
This approach will be discussed briefly in Chapter Three. We
should understand, however, that what is new does not auto-
matically discredit what is older.

MORPHOLOGY

Morphology usually refers to the internal features of words.
Some languages, the American Indian languages among

others, are not word languages; consequently, "morphology" does not have the same meaning when applied to them that it has for a language like English. And even in word languages like English, the boundaries between morphology and syntax are not absolutely clear. For example, in English, linguists make a syntactic distinction between utterances like *The work is complete* and its negative counterpart *The work is not complete*. But speakers may also say, for the negative counterpart, *The work is incomplete,* and then the distinction is generally considered morphological. Although these confusions about the scope of morphology do exist, there are certain basic concepts that give us useful information about the overall structure of word languages. We will now investigate the concepts that will bear directly on the systems explained in the following chapters.

The smallest meaning-bearing unit in a language is a *morpheme*. Words, in English and other word languages, are either single morphemes or are *polymorphemic*. The English word *cat* is a single morpheme that communicates independently of other morphemes and therefore is termed a *free morpheme. Cats* is polymorphemic because it consists of the free morpheme *cat* plus the morpheme for plurality, which in this case takes the form of the phoneme /s/. Since /s/ communicates its meaning by being attached to the free morpheme, it is said to be a *bound morpheme*. Briefly, then, a morpheme may be either of two kinds: free or bound.

Morphemes also carry different types of meaning.[4] Words like *cat, house, walk, idea, pretty,* and *here* belong to a class of morphemes that may be called *message morphemes*. This class includes bound morphemes as well, like the /s/ in *cats* that carries the message of plurality. Words like *the, a, an, and,* and a limited number of others belong to a class called *structural morphemes*. A few bound morphemes like *ful* and *ly* are structural morphemes because, when joined with another morphemic or polymorphemic unit, their primary effect is not to add to the message but to create a functional change. Consider the following examples.

The girl is *pretty*.
The girl performed the dance *prettily*.

The girl is a *beauty*.
The girl is *beautiful*.

We should realize that a given phoneme, like /s/, can be used as more than one bound morpheme. In *The cat's milk is cold* the /s/ carries the message of *possession,* rather than plurality; the context tells the listener which meaning is intended. A similar point is made by the following pairs:

> We *run* to the store.
> He *runs* to the store.
>
> We *dig* for large clams.
> He *digs* for large clams.

Here the /s/ phoneme is used as the *singular* morpheme, to form certain singular versions of the verbs.

Leonard Bloomfield, in his book *Language,* provides a word classification, based on the order and occurrence of free and bound morphemes, that is useful in a brief introduction to morphology:

A. *Secondary words,* containing free forms:
  1. *Compound words,* containing more than one free form: *door-knob, wild-animal-tamer.* The included free forms are the *members* of the compound word: in our examples, the members are the words *door, knob, tamer,* and the phrase *wild animal.*
  2. *Derived secondary words,* containing one free form: *boy-ish, old-maidish.* The included free form is called the *underlying form;* in our examples the underlying forms are the word *boy* and the phrase *old maid.*
B. *Primary words,* not containing a free form:
  1. *Derived primary words,* containing more than one bound form: *re-ceive, de-ceive, con-ceive, re-tain, de-tain, con-tain.*
  2. *Morpheme-words,* consisting of a single (free) morpheme: *man, boy, cut, run, red, big.*[5]

The word *cats,* as we saw, has a bound morpheme, /s/, in a final position, as a *suffix.* Similarly, the word *incomplete* has a bound morpheme, *in,* in an initial position, as a *prefix.* Prefixes and suffixes can be combined under the general term *affix.* We could go on, following Bloomfield, to note that a word like *complete* is itself a combination of bound forms (*com-plete, de-plete, re-plete*). But there is still another variety of bound morpheme, the *alternate-bound,* which we find in words like *geese, teeth, feet, mice, went, bought, was,* and *men.* In these examples the very heart of the original word (*goose, tooth,* etc.) has been altered, to express plurality or past tense.

One other aspect of morphology is important to the concepts presented in this book: the fact that a given morpheme may take the form of any of a number of phonemes or combinations of phonemes. For instance, other phonemes besides /s/ can be used to indicate plurality. Consider the following pairs and the phonemic notation for each suffix:

> *cat* pluralized to *cats* is *cat* + /s/
> *watch* pluralized to *watches* is *watch* + /əz/
> *boy* pluralized to *boys* is *boy* + /z/

And some words have their own peculiar forms. *Child* and its plural *children* not only pluralize in a distinct way, but the addition of the bound morpheme plural brings about a phonetic modification in the base form; that is, *child* rhymes with *wild*, but the *child* of *children* rhymes with *killed*. Regardless of the phonemic shape of a morpheme, each variant form is termed an *allomorph* of that morpheme: /s/, for instance, is one allomorph of the plural morpheme.

SYNTAX

Syntax refers to the extension of phonemic and morphemic units into multiword units traditionally called *phrases, clauses,* and *sentences.* In the sense of a hierarchy, phonemes pattern into morphemes, morphemes may pattern into words, and words may pattern into phrases, clauses, and sentences.

There are two other terms that we should introduce here: *exocentric structure* and *endocentric structure.*[6] Though these terms are used somewhat differently by different linguists, they can be defined for our purposes roughly as follows: an exocentric structure contains the minimum units required to create a complete sentence. For instance, *lions roar* illustrates one type of exocentric structure—the noun-verb type; neither the noun *lions* nor the verb *roar* can be deleted without destroying the sentence. An endocentric structure, on the other hand, is incomplete in itself, and is used to "flesh out" the exocentric structure. The noun *lions* in *lions roar* can be replaced by the endocentric structure *the old toothless lions,* and the verb *roar* can be replaced by another endocentric form, *may have been roaring.* The two endocentric structures fill out the noun and verb positions in the sentence, but neither by itself is a complete sentence.

Exocentric structures in English fall into a small number of types or patterns.[7] To explain English grammar, we need to postulate only four:

noun-verb:	Jack ran.
noun-verb-noun:	Jack bought a book.
	Jack was president.
noun-verb-adjective:	Jack was handsome.
	Doors slam shut.
noun-verb-adverb:	Jack walked quickly.

Other patterns can be identified, but recent syntactic systems usually treat the others as expansions or *transformations* of the basic four. Transformations, which will be discussed in detail in Chapter Three, are additions to, deletions from, or reorderings of basic exocentric order.

Since the exocentric types are few in number, it is possible to argue convincingly that they are a primary signaling system —that, indeed, we communicate because we structure and perceive, at the syntactic level, within a limited number of basic patterns. From this point on, the minimum basic exocentric patterns will be called simply *base patterns*.

Utterance

Earlier in this chapter we drew some parallels based on the competence-performance distinction. We noted that performance corresponds to the actual utterances of speakers and that investigating these utterances is the method employed by the structural linguist in attempting to describe language systems. It should be apparent that a first step for the structural linguist is to define the term *utterance*. For purposes of this discussion, we will use "utterance" for all morphological structures that speakers use to communicate. Charles Carpenter Fries, in his book *The Structure of English,* provides adequate support for such reasoning. Fries states:

> The easiest unit in conversation to be marked with certainty was the talk of one person until he ceased, and another began. This unit was given the name "utterance." In this book, then, the two-word phrase *utterance unit* will mean any stretch of speech by one person before which there was silence on his part and after which there was also silence on his part. Utterance units are thus those chunks of talk that are marked off by a shift of speaker.[8]

John P. Hughes, in his book *The Science of Language,* proposes that Fries' definition may be reduced to *"an amount of speech put forth by a single person before and after which there is maximum silence."*[9] We may accept the latter definition and note, as do both linguists, that any such definition of "utterance" proves troublesome. Implicit in it is the absence of clearly definable limits. On the one hand, an utterance may be as short as one word—for instance, the answer "No," following a question. On the other hand, an utterance may be thousands of words: everything said by a senator filibustering for hours, perhaps for days; this textbook read aloud from the first word to the last; in short, any single person speaking *ad infinitum.*

The difficulties become even more evident when we try to define "maximum silence." Maximum silence, according to Hughes, "is to be defined as any interruption of speech by a silence (on the speaker's part) which is either, for practical purposes, infinite, or at any rate longer than any one of the other pauses observed during the course of speech."[10] Both Fries and Hughes point out that in conversation it is relatively easy to determine points of maximum silence. By placing terminal juncture symbols, either / # / or /\/, we may note such points in the following example:

/ # / Will I see you this afternoon? / # / (Speaker One noticing his companion's preparations to leave)
/ # / No. / # / (Speaker Two answering)

In each case the utterance is preceded and followed by maximum silence. Both speakers were perhaps reading, meditating, or whatever in silence for some time before the interchange. Problems arise when an attempt is made to identify with any degree of certainty points of maximum silence in single-speaker utterances of considerable duration. And only by identifying such points can the structuralist perceive consistent patterns that will enable him to posit a model grammar. Hughes offers a concept that places utterance in a perspective that controls the highly varied nature of the concept of utterance.

IMMEDIATE AND TRANSFERRED UTTERANCE

One way out of the difficulties is pointed out by Hughes, who states, "Failure to take account of the difference between

immediate and transferred situation has needlessly complicated the systems of syntactic analysis proposed by some
linguists."[11] This remark suggests a reclassification of the
rather nebulous term *utterance* into *immediate utterance*
and *transferred utterance*. Stated somewhat simply, the immediacy of a situation permits speakers to use fragmentary
groups of related words (endocentric structures, in our earlier
terminology) with considerable ease: the situation substitutes
for linguistic elements. When, however, the situation is not
immediately apparent, speakers rely more heavily on linguistic material: they transfer the situation into a verbalized
form.

Imagine, for illustration, that two men are leaning on a
railing surrounding a racetrack that has both a long and a
short oval. Man *A* surveys the scene about him and remarks
to Man *B*, "Where is the red gelding at the moment?" (Re-
member that both men are immediately within the situation,
recognizing and responding to all that the immediate moment offers as extra-language signals.) Man *B* replies, "Running the long track." In the immediacy of the situation,
communication is complete. Man *B* has used a related-word
utterance or endocentric structure that is fully informative,
though it does not have all the linguistic forms that speakers
associate with a sentence.

If, at another time, a speaker tried to recreate the above
situation, he would find that the same fragmentary word
group might be part of his statement, but that his communication would have to be aided by additional linguistic forms.
The speaker might say, "Two men were leaning on a railing
of a racetrack in the early light of dawn. The track had two
courses—one was a long oval and the other a short oval. The
two men were at the track because they were both interested
in the performance of a certain red gelding. The larger of the
two men had arrived at the track slightly before the other
man. It was natural that the smaller man immediately ques-
tioned the larger about the whereabouts of the horse. The
larger man told him that the horse was running the long
track."

By classifying utterance into two distinct types, we can also
account for the fragmented structures that writers sometimes
use: if the context of a work supplies the full situation, complete linguistic forms are not necessary. More important, our

separation of the two sorts of utterance helps us to pinpoint the proper area for investigation: if we want to build a descriptive system of language, we should focus on transferred utterance, in which speakers approach maximum use of linguistic material.

We can sum up our ideas about utterance in a set of schematic rules:

$$\text{utterance} \rightarrow \left\{ \begin{array}{l} \text{immediate utterance} \\ \text{transferred utterance} \end{array} \right\}$$

immediate → language + situation
transferred → sentence, symbolized S

The arrow in each of these rules means "can be rewritten as." The next step is the rewriting of the sentence S itself, in terms of its components, the *noun phrase* and *verb phrase:*

$$S \rightarrow NP + VP$$

This is only a different way of approaching the "base patterns" that we mentioned earlier. We will proceed from this point in Chapter Three.

Summary

The concepts presented in this chapter were selected because they are fundamental to any understanding of language and linguistic research. We should briefly review the importance of a few of them.

1. The definition of language, with its insistence on vocal primacy, leads to a distinction between *competence* and *performance* that initially identifies two important directions in linguistic research: *structuralism* and *generative-transformationalism.*

2. The functional definition of *grammar* indicates the *phonological, morphological,* and *syntactical* components that interact to create language.

3. The questions that follow provide a checklist for understanding some of the other important terms.

a) What is the difference between a *phone* and a *phoneme?*

b) Why are *phonemes* divided into *segmental* and *suprasegmental?*

c) What examples can be given to illustrate the differences among *free, bound,* and *alternate-bound morphemes*?

d) How does the description of *endocentric* and *exocentric* structures lead to the concept of *base patterns*?

e) How do base patterns support the idea of the basic simplicity of a language?

f) What is the relationship between base patterns and *transformations*?

Notes

1. I am indebted to my students, Tipawan Lachawanich and Chantrbhen Patananawin, both of Bangkok, Thailand, and Toshio Takahasi of Osaka, Japan, for making available and verifying the references to Thai and Japanese. The examples of the Thai language are as represented in *A Contrastive Study of English and Thai* by Pongsri Lekawatana *et al.,* prepared for the Defense Language Institute under Aerospace Medical Contract number F 41689-69-C-0004, The Department of Linguistics, The University of Michigan, 1968–1969, and mimeographed at The English Language Center, Bangkok, Thailand.

   The phonetic representations of Japanese were prepared by Toshio Takahasi.

2. Noam Chomsky, *Aspects of the Theory of Syntax* (Cambridge, Mass.: M.I.T. Press,

1965), pp. 10–18. (Covers competence-performance and the components of grammar.)

3. Phonemic symbols are from the Smith-Trager system in George L. Trager and Henry Lee Smith, *An Outline of English Structure* (Norman, Okla.: Studies in Linguistics, Occasional Papers, 3, 1951).

4. We should understand that many linguistic difficulties arise when we try to define the meaning of *meaning*. The term is used here in the general sense of "communication."

5. New York: Holt, Rinehart and Winston, 1933, p. 209.

6. Cf. Bloomfield, pp. 194–196.

7. Bloomfield, p. 194.

8. New York: Harcourt, Brace, 1952, p. 23.

9. New York: Random House, 1962, p. 146.

10. Hughes, p. 146.

11. Hughes, p. 157.

Suggested Readings

Note: Complete bibliographic information for each entry appears in Appendix C: Selected Bibliography.

Bloomfield, Leonard, *Language,* 1933, Chapter 2, "The Uses of

Language," pp. 21–41; Chapter 5, "The Phoneme," pp. 74–92; and Chapter 6, "Types of Phonemes," pp. 93–108.

Bolinger, Dwight, *Aspects of Language*, 1968, Chapter 4, "Structure in Language: The Units of Sound," pp. 38–50, and Chapter 9, "Dialect," pp. 135–155.

Dinneen, Francis P., *An Introduction to General Linguistics*, 1967, Chapter 1, "Linguistics As a Scientific Study of Language," pp. 1–19.

Francis, W. Nelson, *The Structure of American English*, 1958, Chapter 3, "The Significant Sounds of Speech: Phonemics," pp. 119–161.

Fries, Charles Carpenter, *The Structure of English*, 1952, Chapter 2, "What Is a Sentence?" pp. 9–28.

Gleason, H. A., Jr., *An Introduction to Descriptive Linguistics*, revised edition, 1961, Chapter 8, "Outline of English Morphology," pp. 92–110.

————, *Linguistics and English Grammar*, 1965, Chapter 2, "The Origins of Modern Linguistics," pp. 28–47.

Hughes, John P., *The Science of Language*, 1962, Chapter 9, "The Structure of Transferred Utterances, 1. 'Immediate and Transferred Utterances,' " p. 156 and pp. 157–167.

Lloyd, Donald J., and Harry R. Warfel, *American English in Its Cultural Setting*, 1965, Part I, "Language, Man, and Society," pp. 9–77.

Stevens, Martin, "Modes of Utterance," *College Composition and Communication*, May 1963, 65–72.

Trager, George L., and Henry Lee Smith, *An Outline of English Structure*, 1951, Part I, "Phonology," pp. 11–52.

Wardhaugh, Ronald, *Introduction to Linguistics*, 1972, Chapter 4, "Phonology," pp. 68–78.

TWO

Structural Concepts

Chapter One presented an overview of important basic linguistic concepts. From these concepts, it should be apparent that *selection* and *arrangement* are fundamental to linguistic performance. In selecting, English speakers choose from a limited number of phonemes, morphemes, and base patterns. In arranging, English speakers pattern phonemes into two kinds of morphemes and vary four base patterns to give shape to complex utterances. Though this brief summary is obviously simplistic in respect to the total language system, it does indicate why further investigation into modes of selection and arrangement is the substance of structural linguistics.

Given the utterance *the boy saw the man,* the linguist needs to account for the fact that such an utterance communicates while *the saw man the boy* does not. Why is it, the linguist must ask, that word units like *to town, an elephant, may be playing* satisfy the speaker-hearer's sense of language, but word units like *town to, elephant an,* and *playing be may* do not? Thinking back to our earlier discussions, we may say that *the saw man the boy* does not follow a base pattern; that *town to, elephant an,* and *playing be may* are not endocentric structures. These answers are meaningful, of course, only if we consider the principle which controls the selections and arrangements that create base patterns and endocentric structures. These selections and arrangements relate to the concept of *immediate constituents.*

20

Immediate Constituents

We can illustrate two essential features of immediate constituents (IC's) by the following progression:

1. *Boy* is a free morpheme.
2. *s*, phonemically /z/, is a bound morpheme.
3. *Boys* is an English polymorphemic word.
4. *Sboy* uses the same morphemes as *boys* but is not an English word.
5. Thus only when *boy* is immediately next to /z/ in the pattern *boy* + /z/ do English speakers accept the resulting form as a word.

In referring to "immediate constituents," therefore, we imply first of all the need for both immediate juxtaposition and proper ordering of morphemes within a word.

To show that selection is as important as arrangement, we can use the plural allomorphs /s/, /z/, and /əz/. Investigation shows that the /s/ allomorph is the IC with words ending in consonants like /p t k/, the /z/ allomorph is the IC with words ending in consonants like /b d g/, and the /əz/ allomorph is the IC with words ending in forms like /s š c č z ž/.

By observing the IC principle, the linguist may draw many important conclusions about word acquisition, and formation. A word such as *incomplete* shows an IC construction analogous to those of words such as *inappropriate, insufficient, incoherent, incombustible,* and *indifferent.* It seems reasonable to assume that users of English, knowing the negative denotation of *incomplete,* sense the negative meanings of other words with similar IC constructions of *in* + word. Speakers of the language may even create topical words by the same use of analogy within the IC concept; for example, *political spying* brings forth *Watergating* in much the same way that *McCarthyism* developed by analogy from words like *romanticism, Nazism,* and *fascism.* Speakers also create many new words by compounding free morphemes. At some point, speakers compounded *black* and *bird* to create *blackbird, straw* and *flower* to create *strawflower, sun* and *flower* to create *sunflower,* and so forth. Analogies and compounds are only two of a number of ways new words enter the lexicon. The history of word derivation and word form and meaning changes is abundantly documented in *The Oxford English Dictionary*—a linguistic source everyone concerned with English should investigate.

Each of the above examples illustrates the IC principle at the word level. Since syntax is the encapsulating system in the hierarchy of systems, we should now investigate how the IC principle applies to base patterns.

In Chapter One we identified the components that constitute the four minimum base patterns:

> noun-verb
> noun-verb-noun
> noun-verb-adjective
> noun-verb-adverb

Linguists often analyze these patterns by making up an example and then substituting other linguistic elements for each of the components in the example. This procedure of substitution is termed *commutation*. By substituting within utterances, the linguist is able to view layers of syntactic unity and to determine that within each layer the IC's are generally two in number. Some sample base patterns should illustrate the procedure of commutation and the binary nature of IC's.

1. Noun-verb, *Jack ran:* At the word level, this structure consists of the noun *Jack* + the verb *ran*. *Jack ran* is a minimum two-word structure that communicates. Commutation shows that speakers may substitute properly selected forms for either constituent:

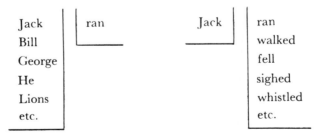

Jack	ran	Jack	ran
Bill			walked
George			fell
He			sighed
Lions			whistled
etc.			etc.

Other two-word structures like *so long, in town, oh boy!* communicate only if considered as immediate utterance.

2. Noun-verb-noun, *Jack bought books:* This is a minimum three-word structure. At the first layer, it consists of the IC's

Jack + bought books. Again, the IC's are two because a speaker may substitute a properly selected word for *Jack* and a properly selected morphological structure for *bought books.*

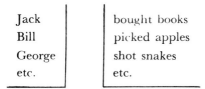

And while the first component, *Jack,* does not contain an IC relationship within itself, the structures *bought books,* etc., include another IC layer which commutation makes evident:

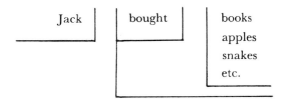

3. Noun-verb-adjective, *Jack was handsome:* This minimum three-word structure shows, at the first IC layer, the same division as number 2. Even though IC division (generally termed "cutting") shows that the second layer patterns the same as the second layer in number 2, commutation within the second layer exhibits that the pattern is distinct:

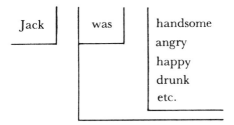

Obviously speakers will accept any of the above three-word structures but will reject *Jack was books, Jack was apples, Jack was snakes.*

4. Noun-verb-adverb, *Jack walked quickly:* This minimum three-word structure shows the same IC cuts as numbers 2

and 3. Commutation again indicates that words which can fill
the second layer must be properly selected:

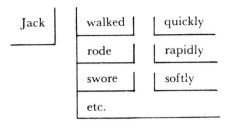

Again, speakers will accept these examples but will reject
Jack walked books, Jack walked apples, and so forth. Some
English speakers may utter *Jack walked handsome, Jack
walked drunk,* etc., but IC investigation at both the word
and utterance levels indicates that proper selection after
verbs like *walked, rode,* and *swore* generally requires the addition of the structural morpheme *ly,* creating, for example:

    Jack walked handsomely
    Jack walked angrily
    Jack walked drunkenly (*drunk + en + ly*)

Each of the four base patterns illustrates the importance of
commutation in assessing IC relationships. The emphasis
given here to *properly selected* relates specifically to the struc-
turalists' procedure of commutation; i.e., a linguistic form is
properly selected if it is commutable into analogous structures.

At this point, we can draw some additional contrasts between structural and generative-transformational designs. IC's
and the procedure of commutation are the basic tools of a
structural grammar that relies on the investigation of *surface
structures* (performance) to draw conclusions about arrangement and selection of lexical features. In contrast, a generative-transformational grammar proposes rules, based on the
speaker-listener's competence, that provide an analogue for
the *deep structures,* including the lexical, that are part of the
speaker-listener's knowledge of the underlying structure of
his language.

As an illustration of deep structure, consider the following
puzzle: why is *Jack bought snakes* an acceptable English utterance while *snakes bought Jack* is not? If we assign to the

verb *buy* a lexical notation that it and its forms are +human and assign to the noun *snake* a lexical notation that it and its forms are ⁻human, we begin to answer the question. We can then establish a syntactic noun-verb-noun description that specifies a [+noun, +human] [+verb, +human] [+noun, ⁻human] pattern. Such a pattern may generate:

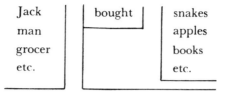

Jack	bought	snakes
man		apples
grocer		books
etc.		etc.

The pattern does not permit *snakes bought Jack, apples bought Jack, books bought Jack,* etc. The +human and ⁻human notations are called *lexical entries,* because they, along with the words to which they apply, will be listed in the lexicon of the language. They reflect the *semantic* or "meaning" composition of the words in the lexicon, and for that reason are part of the deep structure.

It is important to make these points now because they prepare the way for the discussion in Chapter Three of the concepts that support generative-transformational or Gt grammars, as they shall henceforth be called. Establishing form classes and function words is also pertinent to both structural and Gt grammars.

Form Classes

The lexicon of the English language consists of two kinds of words, often termed *empty* and *full.* About 300 of our words are empty words, so termed because they do not have a referent outside the language. *The, a,* and *an* are examples. Structural grammarians call such free structural morphemes *function words.* Most of the words in our lexicon, however, are full words, ones that have a referent outside the language. That is to say, the word *book* refers to a combination of paper and printed matter that English speakers verbalize with the word symbol *book.* In a similar manner, the word *run* refers to an action whose consistent verbal symbolism is accepted

by the community of speakers. Words like these two examples
are classified into groups called *form classes*. We will establish
form classes before investigating function words.

At the outset, it is important to make two observations.
First, form classes identify both words and endocentric structures. Second, a form class, though not definable, is describable
because it functions in a syntactic position and has certain
other describable characteristics. In the preceding section
we identified the minimum base patterns by noting the form-
class words—noun, verb, adjective, and adverb—which comprise the syntactic order.

FORM CLASS I

The *nominal* or *noun* class (N) includes all words and
endocentric structures that can substitute for the first word in
the two-word base pattern. Taking up our example *lions roar,*
let us consider possible substitutes for the noun *lions:*

> people, moving, mice, tall,
> the little child, a moving van, sincerely

English speakers will quickly state that *moving, tall,* and
sincerely cannot be substituted for *lions;* therefore these forms
are not in the nominal class. But *people, mice, the little child,*
and *a moving van* will substitute for *lions,* because each can
be placed in the same IC relationship to a form of *roar. People* and *mice* fit the pattern without alteration. *The little
child* and *a moving van* fit the pattern if *roar* is changed to
roars. The overall commutation procedure remains valid since
there is another pattern, *a lion roars,* into which *the little
child* and *a moving van* may substitute.

In addition, these substitutable words and endocentric
structures have certain characteristics which complement their
identification as N. For example, words classified as nouns
may take plural and possessive morphemes. *Mice* is a plural
alternate-bound form that may take a possessive affix and
become *mice's.* Endocentric structures that pattern as N are
generally characterized by the inclusion of a noun word; for
example, *the little child* and *a moving van* both contain noun
words.

The nominal form class also includes a set of words termed
pronouns. Although pronouns may fill the N form-class posi-

tion in a pattern, they are quite different from nouns in their morphological composition. Because they vary widely in respect to morphological considerations such as singular, plural, and possessive forms and because some pronouns bear *case* designations—that is, are restricted to certain N positions—it is best to classify them according to kinds and mention some of their variant morphological characteristics.

Pronouns may be designated as *personal, relative, interrogative,* and *reflexive*. A list of personal pronouns like *I, we, he, she, his, her, me, us, they, it, them, mine*, etc., indicates that some (*I, he, she*) are singular *nominative case* and some (*me, her*) are singular *objective case; you* may be either singular or plural and either nominative or objective case; *it* is singular but may be either nominative or objective case. *We* and *they* are plural nominative case, and *us* and *them* are plural objective case. *His* and *mine* are two of a set that are *possessive case,* but we will deal with them differently in the following section. Words like *everyone, somebody, someone,* etc., which do not take different case forms, may be classified as *indefinite* personal forms. Some sample patterns may better illustrate singular, plural, and case:

> *I see him: I* is singular nominative; *him* is singular objective.
>
> *he sees us: he* is singular nominative; *us* is plural objective.
>
> *we see you: we* is plural nominative; *you* may be either singular or plural objective but may also be singular or plural nominative in the pattern *you see me.*
>
> *I see it: it* is singular objective but may also be singular nominative in the pattern *it sees me.*

These patterns indicate that *me see he,* for one example, is unacceptable. Case considerations are remnants from the Old English period when the language was fully inflecting—that is, when case affixes determined the function of nouns, pronouns, and adjectives and when other bound morphemes determined the formation and patterning of other word forms.

The forms of the relative and interrogative pronouns overlap. *Who, whom, whose, which, what,* and *that* belong to the relative category, and all of these except *that* are also interrogative. Relative pronouns normally head accumulated word groups like the following:

> The boy (*who* mowed the lawn) is my son.
> You bought the car (*that* I sold).
> I know (*what* you bought).

Interrogative pronouns normally head questions: *who are you? whose is this book?* and so forth. In addition to the possessive case *whose,* only *who* and *whom* retain a case consideration, and that is mostly overlooked by speakers: *whom did you see?* is most often *who did you see?* A lexical entry shows that *who* and *whom* are +human, that *which* is ⁻human, and that *whose, what,* and *that* are either +human or ⁻human.

Reflexive pronouns are combinations of certain personal pronouns and the bound forms *self* and *selves.* Note the singular and plural forms in the following examples:

singular	*plural*
myself	ourselves
himself	themselves
herself	
itself	

Instead of saying *I bought the book for me,* speakers may say *I bought the book for myself* or *I bought myself the book;* and they may clarify a possible ambiguity in *John bought the book for John* by saying *John bought the book for himself* or *John bought himself the book.*

In summary, the N or nominal form class contains three kinds of units: nouns; pronouns; and endocentric structures that themselves contain nouns or pronouns or both. We can explain the similarities and differences between nouns and pronouns as follows. Syntactically they both belong to the N form class because each fills the N position in a base pattern. Morphologically they are different: *lion* is a noun because it can take plural and possessive affixes, while *he* is a pronoun because it is part of a group of words that share different and unique morphological characteristics.

FORM CLASS II

The *verbal* or *verb* class (V) includes all words and endocentric structures that can substitute for the second word in the two-word base pattern. Consider the following possible substitutes for *roar* in *lions roar.*

> runs, eating, wood, talk, moved, better, could eat, did run, may have been eating, can talk

English speakers will eliminate the words *wood* and *better* and will also sense that *runs* and *eating* do not substitute into the pattern *lions roar. A lion roars* provides a structure into which *runs* commutes, but *eating* by itself cannot commute into any base pattern structure. It does, though, become part of the V form class in V endocentric structures such as *may have been eating;* it is composed of a verb form, *eat,* plus an affix, *ing.* Morphologically, the word *eating* may be considered a verb because verbs take bound or alternate-bound morphemes that indicate verb *singular,* verb *past,* verb *past participle* and *present participle*—for example, *eats, ate, eaten,* and *eating.*

Syntactically, V endocentric structures take many forms that will substitute into the base pattern. Some were in the foregoing list. Others are:

Lions	do eat
	did eat
	shall eat
	should eat
	may eat
	might eat
	shall have been eating
	could have eaten
	etc.

FORM CLASS III

The *adjectival* or *adjective* class (adj) includes words and endocentric structures that substitute for the third word in a three-word base pattern like *Jack was handsome.* Many adjectives may pattern with nouns into endocentric structures like *handsome Jack, pretty girl,* and *beautiful trees.* Adjectival endocentric structures can generally fill the N position as well as the adj position.

Morphologically, adjectives may take bound morphemes that indicate *comparative* and *superlative* degrees; *hot, hotter,* and *hottest* are an example of a sort of "regular" addition of affixes to create comparative and superlative. Some adjectives form these degrees by alternate-bound forms; for instance, *good, better, best,* and *bad, worse, worst.* Young children and some dialect speakers, having heard the "regular" forms, often create *good, gooder, goodest,* and *bad, badder, baddest* by analogy. "Worser" is not uncommon in English speech, nor is the formation of comparative and superlative where none can logically exist: *he is deader than a doornail* and *that's the deadest party I've ever been to* suggest degrees of *dead* which are inane but which are highly descriptive. Obviously adjectivals add much to a language.

FORM CLASS IV

The *adverbial* or *adverb* class (adv) consists of words and endocentric structures which can substitute for the third word in a three-word pattern like *Jack ran quickly.* The procedure of commutation again shows the IC relationship in a wide variety of forms:

> he spoke *softly (loudly, rapidly)*
> people are *here (there, at the park)*
> he arrived *yesterday (today, before noon)*
> he went *to town (to work, to the park)*
> electricians work *well (diligently, hard)*

Certain words are adverbs because they perform as *intensifiers* of other adverbials or adjectivals. For example, *electricians work well* may be made more emphatic by the addition of the intensifier *extremely: electricians work extremely well.*

Morphologically, only adverbs ending in the morpheme *ly* lend themselves to statements about their composition. We may distinguish these by stating that they do *not* take comparative and superlative affixes. For instance, the adjective *quick* can become *quicker* and *quickest,* but the adverb *quickly* cannot become *quicklier* or *quickliest.*

It should be emphasized that accurate identification of a form class is dependent on consideration of *both* the syntactic properties—the placement within base patterns and the possible combinations with other words to form endocentric structures—and the morphological characteristics. From a purely structural viewpoint, the morphological composition, once identified, is of minimal importance. Morphological composition is pertinent, however, to the design of a Gt syntax. We will pursue this pertinence later.

Function Words

Words such as *the, an, a, this, by,* and *of* are representative of the function words or empty words, the ones that do not have a referent outside the language. Although these words are relatively few in number, they have a vital influence on English utterance. The importance of function words can be illustrated by comparing the quality of utterances not having them with that of utterances including them. Consider the following pair:

> Man rides horse.
> The man rides a horse.

Linguists generally identify three types of function words: *noun determiners, prepositions,* and *conjunctions.* Their functions are to signal the appearance of form-class words and to combine with form-class words to create endocentric structures. Since all three types have *determinant* functions of one sort or another, we will symbolize each one by the capital letter D together with an appropriate lowercase letter: Dn will indicate a noun determiner, Dp a preposition, and Dc a conjunction.[1]

NOUN DETERMINER (Dn)

These words introduce a member of the nominal form class and signal that the resulting endocentric structure performs as N in an utterance. The following are Dn words:

> Articles: *the, a, an*
> Demonstratives: *this, that, these, those*
> Numbers: *one, two, three,* etc.
> Abstract quantities: *many, some, several, few,* etc.
> Combinations of the above: *three of the, some of those, many of the, some of that,* etc.

Within the above classification, there are other features that
can be registered by lexical entries. All Dn's are +human or
−human; *the* is a +definite article; *a* and *an* are −definite;
the is +singular and +plural; *a* and *an* are +singular only;
this and *that* are +singular; *these* and *those* are +plural; and
so forth. Deep-structure rules for the semantic component of
a Gt grammar should note these and other appropriate lexical
features.

The following passage from Bloomfield's *Language* offers
an appropriate segment of language with which to illustrate
noun determiners and the endocentric structures they create.
The notation Dn appears above each noun determiner, and
parentheses enclose each endocentric structure signaled by a
Dn.

    Dn   Dn
(The types of noun expressions) which always have (a

                      Dn
determiner) are preceded, when (no more specific

                   Dn
determiner) is present, by (the articles), definite *the*

                             Dn
and indefinite *a,* whose meaning is merely (the class-

                             Dn
meaning of their respective form-classes). (A grammat-

ical classification), such as definite and indefinite,

                    Dn
which always accompanies (some grammatical feature),

              Dn
. . . is said to be *categoric.* (The definite and indefinite

                             Dn
categories) may be said, in fact, to embrace (the entire

                             Dn
class of English noun expressions), because even (those

types of noun expression) which do not always take

Dn
(a determiner) can be classed as definite or indefi-

nite. . . .[2]

PREPOSITION (Dp)

Like the Dn, these words introduce a noun word or N
endocentric structure which, together with the Dp, constitutes

an endocentric unit that is usually in the adv form class. Many linguistic systems term endocentric structures signaled by Dp's *prepositional phrases.*

By using commutation, we can identify some typical Dp words and note the form class of the resulting prepositional phrase. Consider the following utterances:

1. The rains came after the fire.
2. He saw the bird beside the bush.
3. He left his money at home.
4. Men in motion blurred the photograph.
5. The animal with the zookeeper is rare.

In these sentences, the Dp words are *after, beside, at, in,* and *with. After the fire, beside the bush, at home, in motion,* and *with the zookeeper* are prepositional phrases that pattern as adverbials. Often traditional grammars consider the prepositional phrases in 4 and 5 as adjectivals. But an accurate investigation of base patterns shows that utterances 2 through 5 are composed of *multiple base patterns:*

2. He saw the bird beside the bush.
    (he saw the bird) (the bird is beside the bush)

3. He left his money at home.
    (he left money) (the money is at home)
    (he possesses money)

4. Men in motion blurred the photograph.
    (men blurred the photograph) (men are in motion)

5. The animal with the zookeeper is rare.
    (the animal is rare)
    (the animal is with the zookeeper)

We should mention that the multiple base patterns are abstractions. We cannot be certain of the precise form a speaker may give to each; but we should observe that these base patterns are deep-structure syntactic components which through transformations create the surface-structure utterances. We will have more to say about syntactic deep structure, as well as lexical deep structure, in Chapter Three.

The word *to* functions in constructions other than the prepositional phrase. *To* is a Dp in the utterance *He went to town* but serves a special function in the utterance *He went to see the town.* In the latter, *to* is an IC adjoined to *see,* a

A New English Primer

word that is in the V form class. The IC relationship *to* + V creates a construction called an *infinitive*. We will indicate the determinant function of *to* in this relationship by calling the *to* a Di. We should note that the construction is symbolized *to* + V rather than *to* + verb because the verbal position can be filled by an endocentric structure:

> She wished to see the town.
> She wished to have seen the town.
> She wished to be seeing the town.
> She wished to have been seeing the town.
> She wished to be seen in the town.
> She wished to have been seen in the town.

To and a few other words that are usually Dp's can also function in another sort of V structure. In the utterances *look for the books, look to the guns, look about the field,* for example, *for, to,* and *about* do not signal a prepositional phrase but have an IC relationship with the preceding V form. Such words in this type of IC construction are termed *particles,* and should be considered part of the total V endocentric structure.

Although the word *of* is listed in dictionaries as a preposition, there is significant structural and historical support for removing it from the Dp category. The word's most obvious use in English is to indicate possession, a concept that is properly a matter of *case.* What we earlier called the possessive case is more accurately termed the *genitive,* especially in reference to nouns. Using this new term, we can say that the structure *horse of the king* is best conceived as *horse* + *the* + *king* + genitive case, rather than as *horse* + prepositional phrase. A comparative example makes the point more clearly. In Old English, possession was indicated by a genitive-case inflection on the noun. And we know that in present-day English, possession can be designated by an apostrophe and *s.* Therefore we have:

> eoh cyning<u>es</u> = the king'<u>s</u> horse = horse <u>of</u> the king

Since *of* is simply a different way of making the same signal as *es* in Old English and *'s* in present-day English, we can legitimately say that *of* is not a true preposition but rather an IC of the genitive case. Besides possession, this case can indicate such things as measurement (*a ton of hay*), source (*fruit of the loom*), and composition (*an avalanche of snow*). We will use the symbol < to designate the genitive *of*, > to designate a possessive affix, and N> to designate a possessive pronoun:

> N   <   N
> The idiosyncracies of elephants are legendary.

> N   >   N
> The elephant's idiosyncracies are legendary.

> N>   N
> His book is on the table.

> N>   N
> She saw her image in the water.

Since this discussion of prepositions (and nonprepositions) has ranged quite widely, a brief summary may be helpful.

1. Prepositions (Dp) signal endocentric structures generally called prepositional phrases. These phrases predominantly pattern as adverbials, though some may pattern as adjectivals.
2. When the word *to* is an IC of a V structure in the order *to* + V, the structure is termed an infinitive and *to* is designated a Di.
3. Some other words that often function as Dp's may instead be particles in a V endocentric structure.
4. The word *of* is not a Dp but, more properly, a signal of the genitive case.

CONJUNCTION (Dc)

These words function as connectors. Words such as *and, but, or, nor* usually join linguistic elements that are alike in form or function:

> N   Dc   N
> Jack and Jill

> adj   Dc   adj   N
> hot and heavy bricks

> Dp   Dc   Dp
> (to the cities) and (to the towns)

> Dc
> I went to the cities and I went to the towns.

> Dc
> He knew (that he lost) and (that he failed).

Some grammars identify three kinds of conjunctions: *co-ordinate,* illustrated by the above examples; *subordinate,* ones that join clauses traditionally termed *dependent* to those termed *independent;* and *correlative,* ones that have two-word forms like *either . . . or* and *neither . . . nor.* But because the terminology is sufficiently vague to prove troublesome, it will not be used in the following explanations of the joining function of Dc forms.

It is best, perhaps, simply to say that conjunctions designate linguistic forms that connect. This generalization will cover Dc forms that serve multiple functions. Relative pronouns, for example, serve both as connectors and as N forms—"function" words and "form-class" words. Sometimes too they contain the possessive.

DcN
There is the duck that walks on his wings.

DcN
I heard what you said.

DcN>
The swan whose wing is black flies high.

This discussion of function words reveals their importance in forming English utterances. We may say that function words are a primary signaling system. For instance, the Dn *a* signals that the N form to follow will be singular and that the endocentric structure will be indefinite rather than definite and that the structure itself will pattern as N in an utterance.

Structural Analysis

The preceding section developed the concepts that are the bases for structural analysis. It should be apparent that the structuralist relies on obtaining a significant *corpus* of a language, which he can then investigate at the phonological, morphological, and syntactical levels in order to discover the significant characteristics that make up its grammar. If the linguist is working with a language that is unknown to him, he must rely on an informant to tell him which features are significant—which sounds distinguish meaning and therefore are the phonemes of the language; which sounds "carry" meaning and therefore are the morphemes of the language; which morphemes pattern into utterances or segments of utterances and therefore indicate the syntax of the language. In each of these areas the principle of immediate constituents is the controlling concept that leads to a description of the language.

Commutation, form-class designations, and function-word designations provide the necessary "tools" for two systems of structural analysis. By dealing with IC's and using marking symbols, we have, in fact, already begun to develop the two systems: *immediate-constituent analysis* and *structural marking symbols*.

IMMEDIATE-CONSTITUENT ANALYSIS

By "cutting" an utterance into IC's, immediate-constituent analysis offers a schematic representation of the layers of structural unity, revealing morphological patterning into words, word patterning into endocentric structures, and endocentric-structure patterning into exocentric structures. Earlier, we noted the binary nature of each IC layer. We can now examine some IC diagrams that demonstrate the characteristic features of an IC analysis system.

1. The small boy ran six miles.

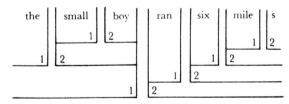

2. A silly clown emerged from the tent.

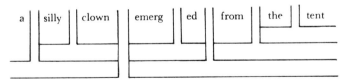

3. The operatic performance was magnificent.

4. The first-line soldiers fired hastily.

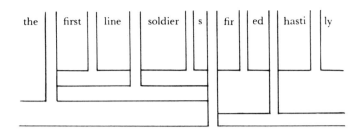

5. The traveling man awoke in the early morning light.

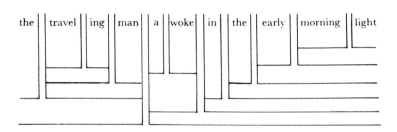

6. The boy with red hair bought a red wagon.

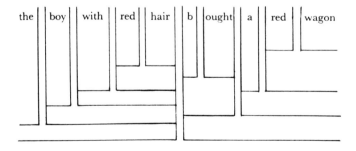

7. The beautiful woman was queen.

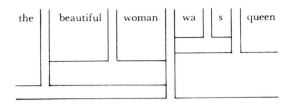

The above examples are relatively uncomplicated utterances that are single base patterns or base patterns in combinations. Some slightly more complex utterances similarly show the layers of syntactic unity and the binary nature of IC's:

8. He is the boy who broke the window.

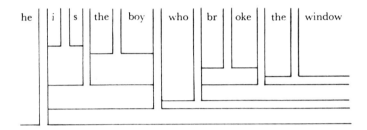

9. I know who saw you.

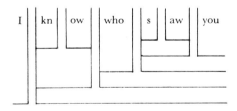

10. To live a good life was his desire.

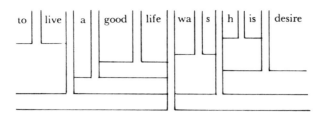

Problems develop when we attempt to perform IC analyses on questions, negatives, and other utterances that show "discontinuity": that is, utterances in which the "regular" IC noun-verb order is reversed or interrupted. It is possible, of course, to adjust the system to these problems, but the adjustment often creates the sort of diagram which in itself may complicate rather than clarify the utterance under consideration. IC analysis shows how morphemes, words, phrases, and clauses combine, but there is nothing in the "cuts" that "tells" us anything about plurality, tense, possession, etc.; and IC analysis does not yield any information about the lexical or phonological characteristics of the formatives or the utterance. Such problems do not, however, diminish the importance of IC relationships, nor do they diminish the sensitivity to structural ordering and unity that IC analysis may develop.

It would be profitable for the student to perform IC analyses on the following sample utterances:

1. His book was lying on the table.
2. The tables beside the desk were large.
3. Library tables are built sturdily.
4. Many libraries have reading rooms.
5. I attended a college that had a large library.
6. The library was the center of intellectual activity.
7. Visiting the library is on the student tour.
8. Study desks lined the walls of the library.
9. Everyone should visit the library when he signs up for the tour.
10. Three people check your books before you leave the building.

STRUCTURAL MARKING SYMBOLS

A structural marking system uses form-class and function-word symbols to demonstrate IC relationships but also to note the nature of the forms that build endocentric structures. By adapting the symbols, we can enlarge the system to indicate other characteristics that differentiate utterances. For instance, an utterance such as *the boy hit the ball* may be marked:

Dn N V Dn N
the boy hit the ball

An utterance such as *that woman was the queen* may be marked in the same way:

Dn N V Dn N
that woman was the queen

Though the two utterances appear to be structurally identical, they are not—a fact that becomes apparent when we attempt to create a passive counterpart for the second utterance. *The boy hit the ball* can be transformed to *the ball was hit by the boy,* but *that woman was the queen* cannot be similarly transformed. On the other hand, *that woman was the queen* can be inverted to *the queen was that woman,* without much change in meaning; but a similar inversion of *the boy hit the ball* creates *the ball hit the boy,* a completely distinct utterance.

A linguist can clarify the distinction between the two utterances in several ways. He can designate the verb *was* as an Lv (linking verb), thus noting that *queen* and *woman* may be inverted without any essential change in the utterance. Other V forms such as *become* and *appear* fit the same pattern. Alternatively, the linguist can use the term *transitive verb* (Vt) to symbolize a V form like *hit,* which takes an N-class "object" that cannot be inverted with the first noun in the utterance; any other type of verb is then called *intransitive* (Vi). Finally, the linguist can represent the N form following the verb as a *noun alternate* (Na) if it can be exchanged with the noun preceding the verb, and as a *noun complement* (Nc) if it cannot be exchanged. We will use the last of these three systems:

Dn N V Dn Nc
the boy hit the ball

    Dn   N   V Dn   Na
    that woman was the queen

In "school" grammar, for lack of a better terminology, the words *not* and *never* are called adverbs. Actually, these words become part of the basic utterance by means of transformation, which we will say more about in the next chapter. For now we can say that *not* and *never* carry the negative message and function as determinants. They can be symbolized by NEG.

We now have a set of symbols, both form-class and function-word, which permit us to construct an analysis system that is to a degree more effective than an IC analysis because it differentiates between form classes and function words and because, with the inclusion of the Na and Nc symbols, it more precisely distinguishes between seemingly similar patterns. Here are some examples of our symbols' use:

      Dn   adj   N   V Dn   N
1. The small boy ran six miles.

      Dn adj   N   V   Dp Dn   N
2. A silly clown emerged from the tent.

      Dn   adj   N   V   adj
3. The operatic performance was magnificent.

      Dn   adj   N   V   adv
4. The first-line soldiers fired hastily.

      Dn   adj   N   V Dp Dn adv   adj   N
5. The traveling man awoke in the early morning light.

      Dn   N   Dp adj N   V   Dn adj   Nc
6. The boy with red hair bought a red wagon.

      Dn   adj   N   V NEG Dn   Na
7. The beautiful woman was not the queen.

      N V Dn   N DcN   V   Dn   Nc
8. He is the boy who broke the window.

      N   V   DcN V   Nc
9. I know who saw you.

      Di   V Dn adj   N   V N>   Na
10. To live a good life was his desire.

This system, like IC analysis, does not tell us about tense, plurality, or the structure of multiword V endocentric structures. But either system allows us to ask questions that may yield additional important information about linguistic performance. In the following list, each question refers to the sample utterance of the same number.

1. Note the form class of the endocentric structures. What do they tell you about the base pattern? Does the answer explain why *miles* is not marked Nc?
2. Note the form class of the endocentric structures. What do they tell you about the base pattern? What might the base patterns of the deep structures be?
3. What might the deep-structure base patterns be? What morpheme can be added to *performance* to prove that it is a noun word?
4. What in the morphological composition of *hastily* indicates that it is an adverb?
5. Although *traveling* is in the adj form class in this utterance, what other form class might it fall into?
6. What is the form class of *with red hair?* What are its possible deep structures?
7. Why is *queen* marked Na?
8. Why is *who* marked with two symbols? What might the deep structures be?
9. If we consider *who saw you* as commutable with an indefinite "something," what is the form class of *who saw you?* Why is the form *who* rather than *whom?*
10. Why is *his* marked with two symbols? What is the Di + V structure termed?

So far the example utterances have been created to demonstrate concepts as simply as possible. But it is both worthwhile and necessary that utterances not created expressly for analysis be examined. Work through the following utterances, using the structural marking symbols. Undoubtedly you will often have to consider more than one concept to explain the analysis.

1. Rolf proceeds to describe the ways in which not only emotional but physical trauma, childhood or sports accidents, etc., can also upset the body-balance. Such accidents lead to a series of bodily compensations, which may give rise to physical limitations and distortions and a feeling of weakness or instability in the body which is then transmitted to mental or emotional states.[3]

2. Along Constitution Avenue, just one block from the Department of Justice in Washington, stands a granite pillared building called the National Archives. Enshrined there, under glass, for all to see, are our Constitution and Declaration of Independence. Thousands view them each week.

On the other side of the world, the body of a man named Lenin lies preserved under glass in a tomb in Moscow, and thousands pass through that shrine also.

In 1955, when I visited Moscow, Joseph Stalin was there under glass with Lenin. But now Stalin has been removed.[4]

3. Another system in language has to do with the sounds that we use when we speak. It is known among linguists as "phonology". We commonly think of the sounds of the language as of two kinds, consonants and vowels. But there are also features of stress and intonation. All these together constitute the phonology. The units are known to many linguists as "phonemes".[5]

4. But as the new century dawned, Garland turned to a world of romantic escapism, set in the High Country of the Rocky Mountains, and dealing with cowboys, Indians, forest rangers, and cattle barons. The bulk of this work showed only a residual interest in social themes, and had little artistic merit. His turn to romanticism after so many years of preaching realism was startling but logical. He approached middle age with little to show for his sacrifices. He acquired a wife and family to support. He loved the adventuresome outdoors so much that he joined the Alaska gold rush in 1898 without a second thought. Disappointed at the passing of social issues he had fought for, a trifle bitter that his work had accomplished so little for reform, he turned frankly for a backward look, seeking in nostalgia the comfort and sense of purpose he could not attain in reform or Realism.[6]

Summary

The structural concepts presented in this chapter are of primary importance to a systematic description of language. Taken in their entirety, these concepts indicate that English is a structure-keyed language; that descriptions of English performance must offer methods for viewing the hierarchy of linguistic patterning at the phonemic, morphemic, and syntactic levels. The major concept that controls structural investigation is that of *immediate constituents*. The procedure of *commutation* of IC's leads to the identification of *form classes* and *function words,* and helps us to understand base patterns and endocentric structures. In the next chapter we will see how base patterns form the beginnings of a Gt system by which the linguist can make general statements about syntactic patterning.

The terms *form class* and *function word* distinguish between the "full" and "empty" words in the English lexicon. Form classes, containing the full words, are termed *nominal* (N), *verbal* (V), *adjectival* (adj), and *adverbial* (adv). Form classes indicate the syntactic position the forms can fill. Words that fill form-class positions can themselves be investigated according to their morphological composition. And there are also *semantic* components that lead us to accompany the words in our lexicon by *lexical entries* like +human or −human, +singular or −singular, +plural or −plural, and so on; these components are part of the *deep structure* that will be more completely elucidated by a Gt syntax.

Function words, the empty words, are *determinants* of endocentric structures; these structures in turn pattern as members of form classes. Function words may be generally classified into three categories: *noun determiner* (Dn), *preposition* (Dp), and *conjunction* (Dc). Some function words require special notations: Di when the word *to* has an IC relationship with a V form, making an *infinitive;* < for the word *of* when it functions in a *genitive-case* sense; and > for the possessive bound morpheme. Some words that are usually Dp's can also function as part of the V endocentric structure; when so used, they are called *particles.* The words *not* and *never* signal a negative transformation and are designated by the symbol NEG.

Immediate-constituent analysis and the use of form-class and function-word symbols in a *structural marking system* are two methods by which the structural linguist investigates the *corpus* of the language so that he can formulate significant statements about linguistic performance.

In this chapter and in Chapter One, whenever appropriate, correspondences between structural grammars and Gt grammars have been noted. These correspondences should emphasize the distinction between competence and performance, discussed in Chapter One, and should prepare the student for an examination of Gt theory and grammars.

Notes

1. Cf. John P. Hughes, *The Science of Language* (New York: Random House, 1962), pp. 161–163.
2. Leonard Bloomfield, *Language* (New York: Holt, Rinehart and Winston, 1933), p. 204.
3. William C. Schutz, *Joy: Expanding Human Awareness* (New York: Grove, 1967), p. 31.
4. Bill Adler, ed., *A New Day: Robert F. Kennedy* (New York:

The New American Library, 1968), p. 28.
5. H. A. Gleason, Jr., *Linguistics and English Grammar* (New York: Holt, Rinehart and Winston, 1965), p. 104.
6. H. Wayne Morgan, ed., *American Writers in Rebellion: From Mark Twain to Dreiser* (New York: Hill and Wang, 1965), p. 98.

Suggested Readings

Note: Complete bibliographic information for each entry appears in Appendix C: Selected Bibliography.

Bloomfield, Leonard, *Language,* 1933, Chapter 15, "Substitution," pp. 247–263, and Chapter 16, "Form-Classes and Lexicon," pp. 264–280.

Bolinger, Dwight, *Aspects of Language,* 1968, "Structural Linguistics," pp. 193–199.

Dinneen, Francis P., *An Introduction to General Linguistics,* 1967, Chapter 3, "Grammar As a Formal System," pp. 47–69.

Francis, W. Nelson, *The Structure of American English,* 1958, Chapter 6, "Grammar, Part II: Syntactic Structures," pp. 291–366.

Fries, Charles Carpenter, *The Structure of English,* 1952, Chapter 8, "Structural Patterns of Sentences," pp. 142–172.

Gleason, H. A., Jr., *An Introduction to Descriptive Linguistics,* revised edition, 1961, Chapter 10, "Immediate Constituents," pp. 128–148.

———, *Linguistics and English Grammar,* 1965, Chapter 4, "English Grammars," pp. 67–88.

Hockett, Charles F., *A Course in Modern Linguistics,* 1958, Chapter 17, "Immediate Constituents," pp. 147–156, and Chapter 18, "Form Classes and Constructions," pp. 157–165.

Lehmann, Winfred P., *Descriptive Linguistics: An Introduction,* 1972, Chapter 7, "Syntax: Processes, Devices and Syntactic Patterns," pp. 109–125.

Wardhaugh, Ronald, *Introduction to Linguistics,* 1972, Chapter 6, "Constituents and Patterns," pp. 79–97.

THREE

Generative-Transformational Grammar

This chapter will present an introduction to generative-transformational grammar which will illuminate the development of Noam Chomsky's theories from the publication of his book *Syntactic Structures* in 1957 to the publication of his enlarged edition of *Language and Mind* in 1972. Naturally, the treatment here will be selective, but it will introduce those major concepts that have influenced Chomsky's interpreters in writing English Gt grammars.

Certain concepts are important to an understanding of Chomsky's "revolution in linguistics."[1] These will be enumerated initially without lengthy explanation and will be more completely explained at appropriate points in the development of this chapter.

1. The generative-transformational system is both a *theory* and a *grammar*. The theory reaches beyond the particular grammar by providing a view of how we acquire language and by enabling the linguist to formulate a universal grammatical model—"universal" in the sense that any language may be accommodated.

2. A primary assumption in Gt theory is that a grammar of a language describes the *sentences* of that language or, more exactly, the underlying processes by which a speaker-listener creates and comprehends sentences. We should note the use of the word *creates* rather than *constructs* or *produces*.[2] The

latter words might give the erroneous impression that a Gt grammar is a mechanical device rather than an analogue for, or symbolic representation of, creative acts.

3. The sentences a Gt grammar creates will be *grammatical*. Grammaticality is determined by the speaker-listener's acceptance of a given sentence as part of his language.

4. The English language is not a finite-state language; that is, the speaker-listener creates and understands an *infinite* number of sentences. Many of them are *unique,* having been neither uttered nor heard before. If a finite-state language existed, the linguist would not need to account for the creative aspect; to make a grammar, he would merely collect and classify the sentences of that language, whatever their number.

5. A speaker-listener's ability to communicate (his performance) is dependent on his intuitive knowledge of the underlying structure of the language (his competence).

6. Although a language itself is not composed of a finite number of sentences, a linguist's descriptive model may contain a *base component* that does have finite characteristics. The base component can be termed *generative* because it will generate the fundamental structures from which an infinite number of sentences can be derived.

7. The derivation of sentences from the base component involves the act of reordering, adding, or deleting or a combination of reordering, adding, and deleting. The ability to perform and understand these creative acts may be termed a *transformational* capacity.

8. The base component may be said to consist of *deep structures* at the phonological, lexical, and syntactic levels. The deep structures, when subjected to transformations, will create the *surface structures* or sentences of the language.

9. The design features of a Gt grammar will specify rules for the base component and rules for the transformational component.

We can preserve a useful chronological viewpoint by designating the design features developed from Chomsky's *Syntactic Structures* as *Gt Grammar I.* We will then examine subsequent changes in Gt theory and grammar design under the heading *Gt Grammar II.*

In this chapter we will examine sentence creation at the single-base level, and in Chapter Four we will expand the explanation to include complicated sentence structures.

Gt Grammar I

Chomsky's initial work proposed a three-part design consisting of phrase-structure rules, transformational rules, and morphophonemic rules.

Phrase-structure analysis describes IC relationships and provides a finite set of rules from which sentences can be derived. Phrase-structure (PS) rules are related to base patterns. Because the characteristic IC relationship in each base pattern is N-V, the first PS rule can be stated in the formula we introduced in Chapter One:

$$S \rightarrow NP + VP$$

Translated, the rule reads: Sentence can be rewritten as noun phrase plus verb phrase. The right half of the formula, NP + VP, is called the *string* which the rule creates. This division into noun phrase and verb phrase is the equivalent of an initial IC "cut." Chomsky also introduces an intonation pattern (IP) into the formula; but since each base pattern is intonationally the same (2-3-1, according to the system explained in Chapter One), we can eliminate the IP from consideration at this time. We should observe that Chomsky translates N and V into *noun* and *verb* rather than into the form-class terms *nominal* and *verbal;* his reason is that morphological composition is important to Gt rule formulation.

Because of the importance of morphological composition, it must be understood that the IC relationship is either NP singular + VP singular or NP plural + VP plural; for example:

NP singular + VP singular = The boy sees the dog
NP plural + VP plural = The boys see the dog

Either of these two strings will permit the creation of an infinite number of sentences of the type traditionally called *declarative.*

In our system we do not have to specify any particular rewrite rule that makes the NP and VP "agree" in number; the need for agreement will be recognized implicitly when the verb is selected. But we will need a rule that specifies such things as tense. A morphological catalog of all the elements in *The boy sees the dog* will help us to see what we must provide for.

the + boy = Dn + N + singular
sees + the dog = Vt + NP
the + dog = Dn + N + singular
sees = present tense + see in the context NP singular

Morphological cataloging is informative, but it reveals nothing about the ordering of the various symbols into a system that can create sentences. However, we can arrive at a skeletal order by combining the morphological catalog and an IC analysis. Consider the sentence *The boy sees the dog* at each IC layer:

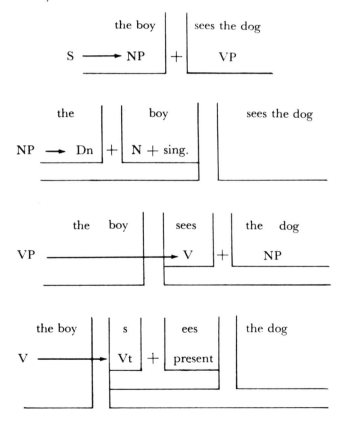

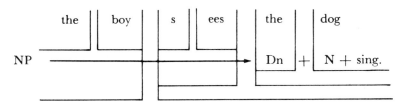

Collecting the symbols in nearly the same order, we can now write a rule which will, when combined with morphophonemic and transformational rules, create *The boy sees the dog* and an infinite number of structurally similar sentences. The rewrite rule is:

S → Dn + N + sing. + present + Vt + Dn + N + sing.

With little difficulty, we can list some sentences that this rule will generate:

The boy sees the dog.
The dog sees the boy.
The boy bites the dog.
The dog bites the boy.
The alligator sees the boy.
The dog bites the alligator.
The boy shoots the alligator.
etc.

Notice that the string can also generate *The alligator shoots the boy* and *The dog shoots the boy* and undoubtedly many others that would seem somewhat odd. Clearly, the model is not yet specific enough to eliminate sentences that, while structurally well-formed, would seem "not quite right" to most English speakers. How do English speakers avoid creating such sentences? According to Chomsky's original theory, the question is a semantic one that cannot be precisely answered by a theory of syntax. Meaning relationships belong to an intuitive semantic knowledge that the speaker-listener possesses—a knowledge that is not part of syntactic ordering but nevertheless has "something" to do with the choice of linguistic elements within syntactic structures. It is fair to state that ambivalence about meaning relationships may be a weakness of Gt Grammar I.

Setting aside this possible weakness for the moment, we can consider how to amplify our rewrite string. We can readily see that the rule S → Dn + N + sing. + present + Vt + Dn + N + sing. will not generate *The boy was handsome, The boys walked quickly,* or *The boy ran.* The rule does not account for adj, adv, or Vi forms. More precisely, it does not permit noun-verb-adjective, noun-verb-adverb, or simply noun-verb base patterns. Indeed, we could spend an infinite amount of time creating sentences to fit the string under examination and still have to find additional infinite amounts of time to create sentences fitting the other three base patterns. And that does not include all the possible sentences that can be *derived* from the four base patterns. (Again we are repeating words like *infinite* and *create;* the significance of this reiteration should by now be well established.)

To use Chomsky's adjective, the generative component can be made more "powerful" by employing certain design features that give us, within the scope of a finite set of rules, the flexibility to generate a variety of phrase-structure strings. From these **PS** strings, we may eventually create sentences that resemble base-pattern utterances.

S → NP + VP
NP → Dn + N
Dn → NULL, the, a, an, this, these, many, few, several
    of these, many of the, etc.

$$N \rightarrow \begin{Bmatrix} \text{noun} \\ \text{proper noun} \\ \text{pers. pronoun} \end{Bmatrix} + \begin{Bmatrix} \text{singular} \\ \text{plural} \end{Bmatrix}$$

noun → boy, dog, table, idea, idiosyncracy, etc.
proper noun → John, Mary, Ms. Jones, Horatio Alger,
    etc.
pers. pronoun → he, she, we, us, everyone, someone, etc.
VP → tense + verbal

$$\text{tense} \rightarrow \begin{Bmatrix} \text{present} \\ \text{past} \end{Bmatrix}$$

$$\text{verbal} \rightarrow (\text{auxiliary}) + \begin{Bmatrix} \text{Vi} \\ \text{Vt} \end{Bmatrix} + \begin{Bmatrix} \text{(NP)} \\ \text{(adj)} \\ \text{(adv)} \end{Bmatrix} + (\text{adv})$$

auxiliary → (modal) + (have + part.) + (be + ing)
modal → may, can, will, shall, must

Vi → be, become, run, appear, etc.
Vt → buy, see, tell, take, give, etc.
adj → beautiful, ugly, difficult, fun, etc.
adv → Dp + NP, here, quickly, well, frequently, to-day, etc.
Dp → about, with, above, in, at, for, etc.

These rules need some explanation. The item "NULL" in the Dn category means essentially that no Dn is chosen. The item "part." listed in the breakdown of the auxiliary stands for "participle," a bound or alternate-bound morpheme such as the *en* in *taken*. The braces { } indicate that only one of the enclosed items will be selected as part of the string. Parentheses indicate that the selection of an item is optional. Consider the rule for the verbal:

$$\text{verbal} \rightarrow (\text{auxiliary}) + \begin{Bmatrix} \text{Vi} \\ \text{Vt} \end{Bmatrix} + \begin{Bmatrix} (\text{NP}) \\ (\text{adj}) \\ (\text{adv}) \end{Bmatrix} + (\text{adv})$$

This rule tells us that the verbal *may* contain an auxiliary, *must* contain either a Vi or a Vt, *may* contain either an NP, an adj, an adv, or *none of the three;* and, if one of the three is selected, the verbal *may* contain an additional adv form. Since the auxiliary (or aux) is optional, all of its forms are also optional.

We might wonder why tense, either present or past, is not considered part of the auxiliary, and why it precedes rather than follows the V form even though a linear structural analysis shows that it is usually either a suffix or an alternate-bound morpheme. The reasons are not arbitrary ones. An English VP in a sentence may be said to have a minimum of two constant morphemes, carrying the message of the V form itself and the message of tense. If the sentence uses additional forms as part of its V endocentric structure, these forms are the auxiliaries; and these forms influence the placement of the tense morpheme. As an illustration, let us try to place tense after the V form. If we use the rule S → Dn + N + sing. + Vt + past + Dn + N + sing., we can select *the + boy* + sing. + *see* + past + *the + dog* + sing. We note that *see* + past will quite properly create *saw*. But if we insert an aux option like *will* into the string—*the + boy* + sing. + *will + see* + past + *the + dog* + sing.—we create *the boy will saw the dog,* an utterance that English speakers would reject as a sentence. The unacceptability becomes even more apparent if all the aux options appear:

the + boy + sing. + will + have + part. + be
+ ing + Vt + past + the + dog + sing.

This string creates *the boy will haven being saw the dog*.

Obviously the initial ordering of elements such as tense is important. But a close examination of our last example will reveal that *re*ordering is also necessary: even if we had put the tense in the right place in that example, we would have created past + *will* + *have* + part. + be + *ing* + Vt, or *would haven being see*. To solve the problem, we must move on from phrase-structure rules to those of transformation. Let us start from the beginning and work up to the point at which transformation becomes imperative.

rule:	S → NP + VP
rule:	NP → Dn + N
string:	Dn + N + VP
rule:	Dn → the
rule:	N → noun + sing.
string:	the + noun + sing. + VP
rule:	noun → boy
string:	the + boy + sing. + VP
rule:	VP → tense + verbal
rule:	tense → past
string:	the + boy + sing. + past + verbal
rule:	verbal → aux + Vt + NP
string:	the + boy + sing. + past + aux + Vt + NP
rule:	aux → (modal) + (have + part.) + (be + ing)
rule:	modal → will
string:	the + boy + sing. + past + will + have + part. + be + ing + Vt + NP
rule:	Vt → see
rule:	NP → Dn + N
rule:	Dn → the
rule:	N → noun + sing.
rule:	noun → dog
string:	the + boy + sing. + past + will + have + part. + be + ing + see + the + dog + sing.

At this point we apply the mandatory *affix transformation*. We must move the participle over to follow *be* and the *ing* over to follow *see;* we should also move "past" to the other side of *will,* to clarify the fact that in word formation it will join with *will.*

the + boy + sing. + will + past + have + be + part. + see + ing + the + dog + sing.

The result is *The boy would have been seeing the dog,* a proper English sentence.

The discussion of morphological composition in the previous chapters makes it quite easy to understand that the speaker selects the proper allomorph for singular or plural noun and verb forms. In the case of noun singulars, the allomorph is a *zero* form; it does not change the phonemic composition of a unit like *boy* + sing. The speaker also chooses the proper allomorph to express *person;* for instance, *The boy sees the dog* requires a /z/ affix on the verb that is not used in *I see the dog.* The bound /z/ to express person is used only on certain present-tense verbs, and only when they appear without aux forms and in the context of a third-person singular noun.

Rules that specify such things as the phonemic composition of word units (e.g., *boy* + sing., *boy* + pl.) and the irregularities of verb-singular formation or verb + affix formation are the *morphophonemic* rules. Most Gt grammars which are based on Chomsky's tripartite construction symbolize the morphophonemic level in a manner that may be termed *morphographemic.* After boundary markers have been used to break the string of forms into word units, the sentence is written graphemically—that is, in spelling symbols, rather than in phoneme symbols. Our sample string is marked off in this way:

the # boy + sing. # will + past # have # be + part. # see + ing # the # dog + sing.

Then the sentence is written graphemically as *The boy would have been seeing the dog.*

Now that we have touched on each of Chomsky's three elements—phrase-structure rules, transformational rules, and morphophonemic-morphographemic rules—we can go on to develop our system a little further. First we should establish more fully the functioning of the affix transformation, which we will now designate T-af. What happens, for instance, when only certain aux options appear in the sentence? Since the

T-af is a mandatory transformation, it naturally influences the creation of all sentences. The following points explain its variations.

1. Tense transforms to follow the modal option. If the modal does not appear, tense follows the first aux option in the string:

    will + past + have + be + part. + see + ing = would have been seeing

    have + past + see + part. = had seen

    be + past + see + ing = was seeing

2. Part. transforms to follow *be*. If *be* + *ing* does not appear, part. transforms to follow the Vi or Vt form:

    have + past + be + part. + see + ing = had been seeing

    have + past + see + part. = had seen

3. The morpheme *ing* transforms to follow the Vi or Vt form whenever *be* + *ing* appears.

Although the choice of (*have* + part.) is entirely optional, it is not possible, in the rules we are discussing, to choose the *have* without the part., or vice versa. Both elements must be selected together. The same is true for (*be* + *ing*). However, we should note that *be* and *have* may serve as V forms in themselves rather than as auxiliaries. Of the following examples, the first and third show *have* and *be* as auxiliaries, and the second and fourth as V forms (*have* as a Vt, *be* as a Vi).

                        I + past + have + part. + see + the + movie + sing.

T-af ⇒ I + have + past + see + part. + the + movie + sing.

                        I had seen the movie.

                        I + past + have + six + penny + pl.

T-af ⇒ I + have + past + six + penny + pl.

                        I had six pennies.

                        I + past + be + ing + go + to + the + movie + sing.

T-af ⇒ I + be + past + go + ing + to + the + movie + sing.

                        I was going to the movie.

I + past + be + at + the + movie + sing.
T-af ⇒   I + be + past + at + the + movie + sing.
I was at the movie.

The double arrow after T-af is the standard symbol for transformation.

As an alternative to the linear representation we have used
so far, we can symbolize the working of rules and strings with
a *tree* diagram. Each of the following trees illustrates the
formation of one of the possible base patterns. The T-af and
morphographemic strings follow each tree.

1.

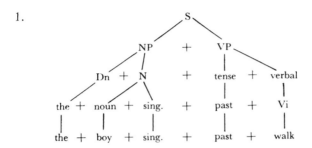

T-af ⇒   the + boy + sing. + walk + past
         # the # boy + sing. # walk + past #
         The boy walked.

2.

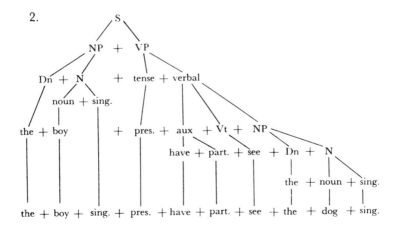

T-af $\Rightarrow$ the + boy + sing. + have + pres. + see +
part. + the + dog + sing.
the # boy + sing. # have + pres. # see
+ part. # the # dog + sing. #
The boy has seen the dog.

3.

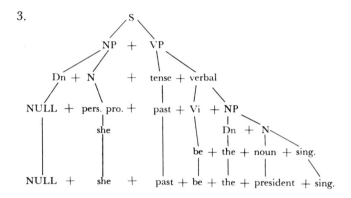

T-af $\Rightarrow$ NULL + she + be + past + the + president + sing.
NULL # she # be + past # the # presi-
dent + sing. #
She was the president.

4.

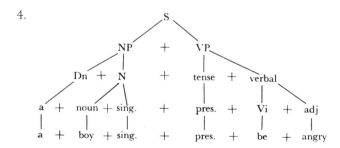

T-af $\Rightarrow$ a + boy + sing. + be + pres. + angry
a # boy + sing. # be + pres. # angry
A boy is angry.

5.

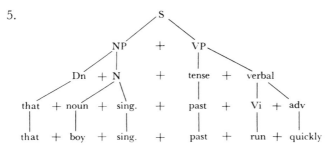

T-af ⇒ that + boy + sing. + run + past + quickly
that # boy + sing. # run + past
quickly #
That boy ran quickly.

6.

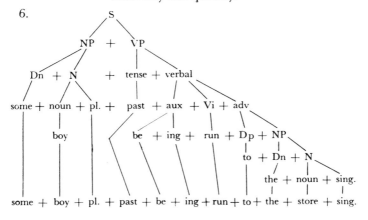

T-af ⇒ some + boy + pl. + be + past + run +
ing + to + the + store + sing.
some # boy + pl. # be + past # run +
ing # to # the # store + sing. #
Some boys were running to the store.

Writing a tree diagram or, for that matter, any sort of linguistic diagram has no intrinsic value in itself. Its value lies
only in relation to the concept or concepts that it may convey.
In this respect, our listing of rules and strings is more informative than a tree diagram because the tree does not indicate
the order in which the rules are applied.[3] Nothing in the
construction of a tree diagram would prevent us from develop-

ing the VP segment before the NP segment; yet proper formation of the VP segment may depend on, at the very least,
singular or plural options in the NP segment. These limitations notwithstanding, the tree is visually more satisfying and
will be accurate if the writer knows the order of the rules.
Actually, once the system is mastered, neither rule-ordering
sequences nor tree diagrams will be necessary; we should at
that point be able to write kernel strings, T-af strings, and
morphographemic strings from our knowledge of the underlying system.

At our present stage, however, practice in writing tree diagrams can be helpful. In working through the following
suggested exercises, the student should try to identify the linguistic elements that are *not* yet accounted for by our grammatical system.

1. Given the rewrite rules below, write trees leading to
strings. Then write the T-af strings, the morphographemic
strings (using the symbol #), and the resulting sentences. Use
only the rules and options noted.

$$S \rightarrow NP + VP$$
$$NP \rightarrow Dn + N$$
$$N \rightarrow noun$$
$$Dn \rightarrow \left\{ \begin{array}{l} the \\ these \end{array} \right\}$$
$$noun \rightarrow \left\{ \begin{array}{l} animal \\ idea \\ house \end{array} \right\} + \left\{ \begin{array}{l} sing. \\ pl. \end{array} \right\}$$
$$VP \rightarrow tense + verbal$$
$$tense \rightarrow past$$
$$verbal \rightarrow aux + Vi + \left\{ \begin{array}{l} adj \\ adv \end{array} \right\}$$
$$aux \rightarrow modal + be + ing$$
$$modal \rightarrow \left\{ \begin{array}{l} can \\ shall \end{array} \right\}$$
$$Vi \rightarrow \left\{ \begin{array}{l} ran \\ be \end{array} \right\}$$
$$adj \rightarrow angry$$
$$adv \rightarrow \left\{ \begin{array}{l} Dp + NP \\ rapidly \end{array} \right\}$$
$$Dp \rightarrow from$$

2. Write the tree, the T-af strings, and the morphographemic strings that will illustrate the formation of each of the following sentences:

a) He could have been rebuilding the boat.
b) Some of the girls were walking to work.
c) Ms. Smith had had difficulties.
d) Swans are elegant.
e) The boy has become a nuisance.

The sentences we can create at this point, whether we represent their formation by tree diagrams or by ordered listings of rules and strings, are called *kernel* sentences. They amount to a sizeable proportion of our everyday English. But the phrase-structure rules, our initial understanding of morphographemics, and the affix transformation cannot explain such commonplace sentences as:

The boy didn't see the dog.
The dog was seen by the boy.
The dog wasn't seen by the boy.
Who didn't see the dog?
Did the boy see the dog?
What did the boy see?
Was the dog seen?
Was the dog quickly seen?
The boy saw himself in the mirrors.
There was a dog.

We can account for these sentences by introducing several new types of transformation: the passive (T-pass), the negative (T-neg), the *do* (T-*do*), the question (T-q, Tq-wh), the adverbial (T-adv), the deletion (T-del), the reflexive (T-reflex), and the *there* (T-*there*). In addition, variations in stress can be explained by intonational transformations (T-emphasis, T-reassertion).

We will discuss these new transformations in the following sections. The reader will see that some attention must be given to the order in which the transformations are applied. Obviously the English language is too varied—too much the speaker's own "creation"—to conform always to a single transformational sequence; but in some cases we would distort a sentence's syntax by applying the transformations out of order.

THE PASSIVE TRANSFORMATION (T-pass)

The boy saw the dog is said to be in the *active voice.* The corresponding sentence in the *passive voice* is *The dog was seen by the boy.* We can derive the passive from the active by transposing the two NP structures, by adding *be* + part. to the V endocentric structure, and by adding the Dp *by* to the string.

$$
\begin{aligned}
&\phantom{\text{T-pass} \Rightarrow}\ \text{the} + \text{boy} + \text{sing.} + \text{past} + \text{see} + \text{the} + \\
&\phantom{\text{T-pass} \Rightarrow}\ \text{dog} + \text{sing.} \\
&\text{T-pass} \Rightarrow\ \text{the} + \text{dog} + \text{sing.} + \text{past} + \text{be} + \text{part.} + \\
&\phantom{\text{T-pass} \Rightarrow}\ \text{see} + \text{by} + \text{the} + \text{boy} + \text{sing.} \\
&\phantom{\text{T-pa}}\text{T-af} \Rightarrow\ \text{the} + \text{dog} + \text{sing.} + \text{be} + \text{past} + \text{see} + \\
&\phantom{\text{T-pass} \Rightarrow}\ \text{part.} + \text{by} + \text{the} + \text{boy} + \text{sing.} \\
&\phantom{\text{T-pass} \Rightarrow}\ \text{\# the \# dog} + \text{sing. \# be} + \text{past \# see} + \\
&\phantom{\text{T-pass} \Rightarrow}\ \text{part. \# by \# the \# boy} + \text{sing. \#} \\
&\phantom{\text{T-pass} \Rightarrow}\ \text{The dog was seen by the boy.}
\end{aligned}
$$

We can write a formal rule for transforming active to passive as follows:

$$\text{NP}_1 + \text{tense} + \text{V} + \text{NP}_2 \Rightarrow \text{NP}_2 + \text{tense} + \text{be} + \text{part.} + \text{V} + \text{Dp} + \text{NP}_1$$

In the following sections we will omit such formal representations, because they can be easily constructed from our sample progressions of strings.

THE NEGATIVE TRANSFORMATION (T-neg)

The speaker-listener creates and understands negative statements as well as the positive ones contained in kernel sentences:

$$
\begin{aligned}
&\phantom{\text{T-neg} \Rightarrow}\ \text{He was home.} \\
&\text{T-neg} \Rightarrow\ \begin{cases} \text{He was never home.} \\ \text{He was not home.} \\ \text{He wasn't home.} \end{cases}
\end{aligned}
$$

These examples indicate that the negative morpheme may be *never, not,* or the contraction *n't,* a phonetic modification of *not.* Historically, *never* is a phonetic modification of *not ever,* and it may be argued that *He was never home* derives from *He was ever home.* But present-day speakers do not normally form the latter sentence, and *never* had morphological status at least as far back as the Old English *næfre*. Therefore we can consider *never* a distinct morpheme in the negative transformation.

A progression showing *not* serves equally well for *never,* since both forms occupy the same syntactic position.

> He + past + be + home
> T-neg ⇒   He + past + be + not + home
> T-af ⇒   He + be + past + not + home
> # He # be + past # not # home #
> He was not home.

The progression for *He wasn't home* calls for a different morphographemic alignment.

> He + past + be + home
> T-neg ⇒   He + past + be + n't + home
> T-af ⇒   He + be + past + n't + home
> # He # be + past + n't # home #

There are many negative sentences that will not derive from the T-neg alone. *He saw the boy* transforms to *He didn't see the boy,* indicating that another transformation, placing *do* in the kernel sentence, is needed.

THE *DO* TRANSFORMATION (T-*do*)

T-*do* serves a supporting function in creating certain negative and interrogative sentences. It also permits the speaker to add emphasis to a declarative sentence. For instance, the speaker may say *He saw the dog* or he may strengthen the sentence by saying *He did see the dog.* Notice that when *do* is added to the kernel sentence, it takes the tense affix. The progression is:

> He + past + see + the + dog + sing.
> T-*do* ⇒   He + past + do + see + the + dog + sing.
> T-af ⇒   He + do + past + see + the + dog + sing.
> # He # do + past # see # the # dog + sing. #

For *He didn't see the dog,* the transformations appear in the following order:

> He + past + see + the + dog + sing.
> T-*do* ⇒   He + past + do + see + the + dog + sing.

T-neg ⇒   He + past + do + n't + see + the + dog
+ sing.
T-af ⇒   He + do + past + n't + see + the + dog
+ sing.
\# He \# do + past + n't \# see \# the \#
dog + sing. \#

The need for ordering the transformations is evident here; if
T-neg were applied before T-*do*, the negative morpheme
would follow *see*, creating *He did see n't the dog*, an utterance
that is obviously unacceptable as a sentence.

THE QUESTION TRANSFORMATIONS (T-q, Tq-wh)

Sentences like *He saw the dog* are the kernels for two different types of question sentence. Examples of the first type are
Did he see the dog? and *Has he seen the dog?* These questions
require a *Yes* or *No* answer, and are created by a transformation called the T-q. The second type of question requires
some other answer: *Who saw the dog? What did he see? When
did he see the dog?* This sort, formed by adding to the T-q a
second transformation called the Tq-wh, is normally headed
by an interrogative pronoun, adjective, or adverb—a *wh-* word
such as *who, what, which, when,* or *where.*

Many English questions require the T-*do* transformation
when the string contains no aux options. For instance, *Did he
see the dog?* could not be asked in "good" English without
the *did* (*do* + past). However, we sometimes hear a structure
such as *Saw he the dog?* from a person who is just learning
English, because many foreign languages do not use any unit
like *do* in forming questions. The following string progressions will illustrate T-q, T-q with T-*do* support, Tq-wh, and
Tq-wh with T-*do* support.

you + pres. + have + part. + see + the +
dog + sing.
T-q ⇒   pres. + have + you + part. + see + the +
dog + sing.
T-af ⇒   have + pres. + you + see + part. + the +
dog + sing.
\# have + pres. \# you \# see + part. \# the
\# dog + sing. \#
Have you seen the dog?

	he + past + see + the + dog + sing.
T-q ⇒	past + he + see + the + dog + sing.
T-*do* ⇒	past + do + he + see + the + dog + sing.
T-af ⇒	do + past + he + see + the + dog + sing.
	# do + past # he # see # the # dog + sing. #
	Did he see the dog?

	"someone" + past + see + the + dog + sing.
T-q ⇒	past + "someone" + see + the + dog + sing.
Tq-wh ⇒	who + past + see + the + dog + sing.
T-af ⇒	who + see + past + the + dog + sing.
	# who # see + past # the # dog + sing. #
	Who saw the dog?

	he + past + see + "something"
T-q ⇒	past + he + see + "something"
T-*do* ⇒	past + do + he + see + "something"
Tq-wh ⇒	what + past + do + he + see
T-af ⇒	what + do + past + he + see
	# what # do + past # he # see #
	What did he see?

We should note that the intonation pattern (IP), which we have omitted from our discussion of trees and strings, changes when a question transformation is applied. Originally 2-3-1, it becomes 2-3-3; in other words, to ask a question we use higher levels of pitch and stress at the end of the sentence, along with rising terminal contour (see p. 10).

With the strings we have listed we can make two other important points. Once again, we can see that the order of the transformations is important. (Try changing the position of Tq-wh in the sequence, and see what kind of utterance results. Note that both the T-q and the Tq-wh transformations require putting an element at the beginning of the string.) We can see too that indefinite words like "someone" and "something" enable us to account for a necessary element in the kernel sentence—an element whose linguistic form is unknown until the speaker is answered.

Tq-wh will create many different questions that we can analyze by the use of indefinite forms. Consider the following questions and the kernel sentence from which each derives:

When did he see the dog?
He saw the dog "sometime."

Where did he see the dog?
He saw the dog "someplace."

Why did he see the dog?
He saw the dog "for some reason."

How will he see the dog?
He will see the dog "somehow."

What will he see?
He will see "something."

T-q and Tq-wh with T-*do*, in the order noted in the sample progressions, will create all of these questions. When combined with T-neg, the question transformations will create such sentences as:

When didn't he see the dog?
Why didn't he see the dog?
What didn't he see?
Didn't he see the dog?

In sentences like these, a string progression will show T-neg after T-*do*:

	he + past + see + the + dog + sing. + "sometime"
T-q ⇒	past + he + see + the + dog + sing. + "sometime"
T-*do* ⇒	past + do + he + see + the + dog + sing. + "sometime"
T-neg ⇒	past + do + n't + he + see + the + dog + sing. + "sometime"
Tq-wh ⇒	when + past + do + n't + he + see + the + dog + sing.
T-af ⇒	when + do + past + n't + he + see + the + dog + sing.
	# when # do + past + n't # he # see # the # dog + sing. #
	When didn't he see the dog?

Since T-pass has already been presented, we can observe transformation order by a progression that combines T-neg, T-q, Tq-wh, and T-pass. For example, a sentence such as *When wasn't the dog seen by the hunters?* shows the following derivation:

	the + hunter + pl. + past + see + the + dog + sing. + "sometime"
T-pass ⇒	the + dog + sing. + past + be + part. + see + by + the + hunter + pl. + "sometime"
T-q ⇒	past + be + the + dog + sing. + part. + see + by + the + hunter + pl. + "sometime"
T-neg ⇒	past + be + n't + the + dog + sing. + part. + see + by + the + hunter + pl. + "sometime"
Tq-wh ⇒	when + past + be + n't + the + dog + sing. + part. + see + by + the + hunter + pl.
T-af ⇒	when + be + past + n't + the + dog + sing. + see + part. + by + the + hunter + pl.
	# when # be + past + n't # the # dog + sing. # see + part. # by # the # hunter + pl. #

At this point, given a sentence, the student should be able to identify the kernel and the transformational acts from which the sentence derives. It may be helpful, though, to introduce a step-by-step method for this kind of analysis. Take the sentence *Why wasn't he at home?* as an example. First, identify the linguistic elements which can *not* be generated by PS rules and the T-af. Note the transformation from which each derives; for instance:

1. The sentence is a question: T-q
2. The sentence begins with *why:* Tq-wh
3. The sentence is negative: T-neg

Now cross out the linguistic elements that enter by these transformations.

Why wasn't he at home?

If the remaining elements are arranged to follow the intonation pattern 2-3-1, *He was at home* emerges as the kernel sentence. Finally, noting the need to order the transformations, we can write the initial string and the subsequent transformational strings, concluding with the mandatory T-af and the morphographemic string.

Some practice may help to synthesize the explanations offered to this point. Write a string progression for each of the following sentences:

1. The hunter didn't find the geese.
2. Where did he look for the geese?
3. Have geese been seen by hunters?
4. Why do people shoot geese?
5. When are you going to the country?

THE ADVERBIAL TRANSFORMATION (T-adv)

In our discussion of base patterns and phrase-structure rules, we have placed adverbials at the end of the sentence. A little thought, however, will convince us that adverbials can appear in many different positions:

He went to town in the morning.
In the morning he went to town.
He rides frequently.
Frequently he rides.
He frequently rides.
The baseball is here.
Here is the baseball.

The reader can write his own string progression to illustrate T-adv.

THE DELETION TRANSFORMATION (T-del)

Besides the addition and reordering of elements, transformation can involve the deletion of one or more elements. Deletion becomes especially important in the derivation of sentences from more than one base component. For now, we will illustrate T-del by two string progressions.

"someone" + past + shovel + the + snow

T-pass ⇒ the + snow + past + be + part. + shovel + by + "someone"

T-del ⇒ the + snow + past + be + part. + shovel

T-af ⇒ the + snow + be + past + shovel + part. # the # snow # be + past # shovel + part. #

he + past + give + the + book + sing. + to + me

T-adv ⇒ he + past + give + to + me + the + book + sing.

T-del ⇒ he + past + give + me + the + book + sing.

T-af ⇒ he + give + past + me + the + book + sing. # he # give + past # me # the # book + sing. #

In the first progression, T-del follows T-pass and creates *The snow was shoveled.* In the second, T-del follows T-adv and removes the Dp *to* from the string, creating *He gave me the book.* We should note that *me* is traditionally called an *indirect object,* but the string progression illustrates that it is actually a transformed adverbial prepositional phrase.

THE REFLEXIVE TRANSFORMATION (T-reflex)

In Chapter Two we identified a unique set of nominal linguistic forms that are called pronouns. Among these, we identified a subset called reflexive pronouns. Since reflexive pronouns are in the objective case, they can perform only certain N functions; for instance, they cannot appear in the pattern NP + VP, but they can appear in a pattern like NP + V + Dp + Dn + N:

John + past + see + John + in + the + mirror + sing.

T-reflex ⇒ John + past + see + himself + in + the + mirror + sing.

T-af ⇒ John + see + past + himself + in + the + mirror + sing.

John # see + past # himself # in # the
mirror + sing.
John saw himself in the mirror.

T- reflex can combine with other transformations:

	Joan + past + give + a + book + sing. + to + Joan
T-reflex ⇨	Joan + past + give + a + book + sing. + to + herself
T-adv ⇨	Joan + past + give + to + herself + a + book + sing.
T-del ⇨	Joan + past + give + herself + a + book + sing.
T-af ⇨	Joan + give + past + herself + a + book + sing.
	# Joan # give + past # herself # a # book + sing. #
	Joan gave herself a book.

As an exercise, determine the transformations that create the following sentences. It may prove worthwhile to list them, giving attention to their relative order.

1. The committee voted itself a stipend.
2. What did the committee vote for itself?
3. Didn't the committee vote itself a stipend?
4. The stipend wasn't voted by the committee for itself.
5. When will the committee vote itself a stipend?

THE *THERE* TRANSFORMATION (T-*there*)

Speakers often begin sentences with the adverb *there* instead of an NP structure. Some such sentences may be accounted for by the T-adv. For instance, it may be correct to assume that *There is a dog* derives from *A dog is there* by way of T-adv. However, it is difficult to analyze *There is morality in the universe* along the same lines. And a sentence like *There is a bird in the bush there* can hardly be considered as a modification of *A bird is in the bush there there*. To make our grammar fully representational, we need to postulate a T-*there*.

morality + present + be + in + the +
universe

T-*there* ⇒   there + present + be + morality + in +
              the + universe

T-af ⇒   there + be + present + morality + in +
              the + universe

              # there # be + present # morality # in
              # the # universe #

There is morality in the universe.

INTONATIONAL TRANSFORMATIONS
(T- emphasis, T-reassertion)

A Gt grammar will specify a number of acts of intonational transformation. Speakers regularly vary *stress* to emphasize different meanings: *He CAN do the work, HE can do the work, He can DO the work,* and so forth. Each example can be accounted for by a transformational rule often called a T-emphasis or a T-reassertion.

The sample single-base transformations presented in this section should provide a conceptual view of Chomsky's early theories. It should be apparent that syntax dominates this kind of Gt grammar. For rules including the semantic part of language, we must turn to Gt Grammar II.

Gt Grammar II

All languages have both a sound system and a meaning system—a duality that affects the development of any descriptive grammar. In our discussion so far, the meaning system of English has been slighted. Morphology, of course, provides some insights into meaning, though these are primarily limited to an "understanding" of the vocabulary and of the linguistic symbols denoting tense, case, number, and so on. And syntax provides significant insights into meaning by describing how vocabulary combines with signals such as tense, case, and number to form patterns that native speakers accept as segments of their languages. But our investigation into the areas of phonology, morphology, and syntax has not yet completely accounted for the rejection by English speakers of a sentence like *Snakes shoot boys*. The "meaning signals" within each word which cause English speakers to reject such sentences must lie at a deeper level than any we have yet uncovered.

It is improbable that even specification at the semantic level could account for every feature of a language, but a Gt grammar which offers a means for describing the semantic component may perhaps be more "powerful" than a grammar dominated by the syntactic component. Emphasis on the semantic component is characteristic of the Gt grammars that have grown out of Chomsky's *Aspects of the Theory of Syntax* (1965). In this section, we will briefly examine the concepts and design features of a Gt grammar based on a phonological component, a syntactic component, *and* a semantic component, all of which interact to create sentences.

Considering *Boys shoot snakes* as grammatical and *Snakes shoot boys* as nongrammatical, we can return to our use of lexical entries, assigning each of the words some semantic qualifications:

$$
\begin{bmatrix} boys \\ +\text{noun} \\ +\text{concrete} \\ +\text{animate} \\ +\text{human} \\ -\text{singular} \end{bmatrix}
\begin{bmatrix} snakes \\ +\text{noun} \\ +\text{concrete} \\ +\text{animate} \\ -\text{human} \\ -\text{singular} \end{bmatrix}
\begin{bmatrix} shoot \\ +\text{verb} \\ +\text{active} \\ +\text{animate} \\ +\text{human} \\ -\text{singular} \end{bmatrix}
$$

Having identified a number of lexical entries, we can then write syntactic rules which assign an order, based on compatible semantic features, to the elements of a string. For example, we can specify that the order of a sentence will be:

$$
\begin{bmatrix} +\text{noun} \\ -\text{singular} \\ +\text{human} \end{bmatrix}
+
\begin{bmatrix} +\text{verb} \\ -\text{singular} \\ +\text{human} \end{bmatrix}
+
\begin{bmatrix} +\text{noun} \\ -\text{singular} \\ -\text{human} \end{bmatrix}
$$

Within this minimum structure, it is now possible to select those vocabulary forms which are consistent with the lexical entries. According to the rule, we cannot select *snakes,* a $-$human noun, to precede *shoot,* a $+$human verb; but we can choose almost any $-$human plural noun to follow the verb: *Boys shoot snakes, Boys shoot bottles, Boys shoot cans, Boys shoot potatoes.* Naturally, almost any $+$human plural noun can fill the position of *boys* in these examples.

Let us now consider *The boys had shot a snake* as it could appear in a syntactic tree that specifies lexical entries:

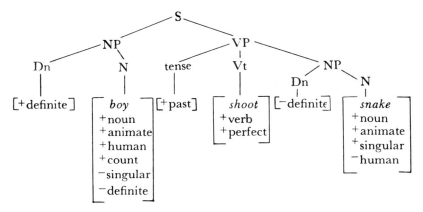

The design illustrated by this combined syntactic-semantic tree allows for transformations within the base-pattern component, in contrast to Gt Grammar I, which uses transformations only after the formation of a kernel-sentence string. For instance, the affix transformation can be accounted for by adding to the lexical entries:

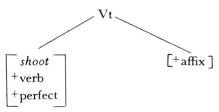

By placing this extra category in the tree and doing the same for other affixes, the system incorporates the T-af within the base component. Using further categories and subcategories of lexical entries, the system can permit other transformations within the base component as well.

Because of this branching of categories and subcategories, the syntactic joining of elements in the system is represented not by plus signs but by a new symbol, as in:

$$S \rightarrow NP \frown aux \frown VP$$

The branching symbol $\frown$ indicates that further subdivision of the elements may occur when the semantic component is specified. Chomsky's model in *Aspects of the Theory of Syn-*

tax^4 shows the following combination of syntactic rules and semantic categories and subcategories.

We may now consider a generative grammar with a base component containing, among many others, the rules and rule schemata (57) and the lexicon (58):

(57) (i) S → NP⌢Predicate-Phrase

(ii) Predicate-Phrase → Aux⌢VP (Place) (Time)

(iii) VP → $\left\{ \begin{array}{l} \text{Copula⌢Predicate} \\ V \left\{ \begin{array}{l} \text{(NP) (Prep-Phrase) (Prep-Phrase) (Manner)} \\ S' \\ \text{Predicate} \end{array} \right\} \end{array} \right\}$

(iv) Predicate → $\left\{ \begin{array}{l} \text{Adjective} \\ (like) \text{ Predicate-Nominal} \end{array} \right\}$

(v) Prep-Phrase → Direction, Duration, Place, Frequency, etc.

(vi) V → CS

(vii) NP → (Det) N (S')

(viii) N → CS

(ix) [+Det —] → [±Count]

(x) [+Count] → [±Animate]

(xi) [+N, + —] → [±Animate]

(xii) [+Animate] → [±Human]

(xiii) [−Count] → [±Abstract]

(xiv) [+V] → CS/α⌢Aux — (Det⌢β) $\left.\right\}$, where α is an N and

(xv) Adjective → CS/α … — $\left.\right\}$ β is an N

(xvi) Aux → Tense (M) (Aspect)

(xvii) Det → (pre-Article⌢of) Article (post-Article)

(xviii) Article → [±Definite]

(58)   (*sincerity*, [+N, +Det —, − Count, +Abstract, ...])

(*boy*, [+N, +Det —, +Count, +Animate, +Human, ...])

(*frighten*, [+V, + — NP, +[+Abstract] Aux — Det [+Animate], +Object-deletion, ...])

(*may*, [+M, ...])

The major difficulty in this kind of system is precise and complete notation of lexical entries. Since words and our understanding of words vary tremendously, how can a finite set of lexical entries be written to encompass all the possible variations? For example, can a reasonably accurate yet manageable set of lexical entries account for the different uses of *shoot* in *Boys shoot snakes, Boys shoot craps,* and *Porcupines shoot quills*? Quite clearly, the system in such cases will fall short of perfection. But by integrating the deep structure semantic and syntactic components, the system can parallel the speaker-listener's creative act more closely than does a purely structural approach or a design like Gt Grammar I.

The system can also allow us to integrate phonological rules with the base component. For instance, we know that certain morphemes, plural and possessive among them, take differing phonemic shapes when combined with various other morphemes. We have called these differing phonemic shapes allomorphs. Our system could be extended to include a phonological component that would specify which of the allomorphs would be used in each possible instance. First we would determine which allomorph seemed the most "regular" or frequent, and we would write a base rule incorporating that one into the pattern; then we would write rules for changing the allomorph according to modifications in its context—rules that would parallel the changes in a speaker's articulation. When completely derived, the phonological component would offer a sequence of phonemes that would approximate the pronunciation of the sentence. But because this book offers only a general introduction to phonology, we cannot develop the matter here.

Summary and Implications

The nine points enumerated in the introductory section of this chapter actually constitute a summary of generative-transformational theory and design. Our sections dealing with Gt Grammars I and II have explained the salient features of these nine points. It is important, however, to emphasize the boundaries of our preceding explanations and to state the implications of Gt theory for a philosophical-psychological approach to language acquisition.

Gt grammars provide a model of the speaker-listener's creative act in forming communication units termed *sentences.* In this chapter, the section on Gt Grammar I presented the finite set of PS rules and some representative transformations for sentences which are characterized by a single base. Gt grammars like Gt Grammar I are dominated by the syntactic component. Questions of meaning relationships in word units —the semantic component—are generally left unspecified.

Designs like Gt Grammar II, based on a recognition of the importance of the semantic component, permit a more accurate representation of the deep structures by which the speaker-listener creates and understands sentences. Gt Grammar II interrelates the phonological, semantic, and syntactic components within the base component. The use of branching rules rather than PS rules permits transformations to take place within the base component. However, it may perhaps be argued that problems of semantic representation and the subsequent complexity of design impair the system's effectiveness.

As a theory of language acquisition, generative-transformationalism is revolutionary. Every part of this chapter has demonstrated that sentence formation is a creative, unique human act. From a finite set of rules (either PS, syntactic-semantic, or semantically dominated[5]) Gt grammar derives an infinite number of sentences.

The theory and the grammar lead us to a certain view of human acquisition of language, a view directly opposed to the notion that language learning is primarily imitative. Since even a young child can create an infinite number of sentences, though they may all be simple ones, we cannot accept the idea that children produce sentences mainly by imitating those they have heard from adults. Instead of learning individual sentences, a child learns the underlying structure of sentences—the sort of structure we have been representing in our grammar. As the child matures, he is able to create an increasing number of patterns from this underlying structure. As a corollary to our theory, we can suggest that a child's progress in learning a language depends more on his maturity than on the amount of exposure he receives to the language. No amount of exposure to sentences will help him much until he is mature enough to grasp the rules by which the sentences are created.

Notes

1. See John Searle, "Chomsky's Revolution in Linguistics," *The New York Review of Books,* 18:12 (June 29, 1972), 16–24.
2. Even though Chomsky uses the term *produces* in *Syntactic Structures,* his presentation as a whole stresses creative aspects.
3. Noam Chomsky, *Syntactic Structures* (The Hague: Mouton, 1957), p. 27.
4. Noam Chomsky, *Aspects of the Theory of Syntax* (Cambridge, Mass.: M.I.T. Press, 1965), pp. 106–107.
5. Recent research has developed some semantically dominated designs that are generally included under the term *generative semantics.*

Suggested Readings

Note: Complete bibliographic information for each entry appears in Appendix C: Selected Bibliography.

Chomsky, Noam, *Aspects of the Theory of Syntax*, 1965.

————, *Cartesian Linguistics*, 1966, "Deep and Surface Structure," pp. 31–51, and "Acquisition and Use of Language," pp. 59–73.

————, *Language and Mind*, enlarged edition, 1972, "Linguistic Contributions to the Study of Mind: Present," pp. 24–64.

————, *Syntactic Structures*, 1957.

————, and Morris Halle, *The Sound Pattern of English*, 1968.

Lewis, M. M., "The Linguistic Development of Children," *Linguistics at Large*, 1971, pp. 197–208. Also in *Language: Introductory Readings*, ed. Virginia P. Clark, Paul A. Eschholz, and Alfred F. Rosa, 1972, pp. 62–71.

Some additional, though quite technical, discussions of the viewpoint presented in this chapter appear in the following:

Chafe, Wallace L., *Meaning and the Structure of Language*, 1970.

Grady, Michael, *Syntax and Semantics of the English Verb Phrase*, 1970.

Katz, Jerrold J., and Paul M. Postal, *An Integrated Theory of Linguistic Descriptions*, 1964.

McNeill, David, *The Acquisition of Language: The Study of Developmental Psycholinguistics*, 1970.

FOUR

The English Sentence

Up until now we have used the word *sentence* without attempting to define it. Reviewing what we know about the sentence, we can say that it has a characteristic IC structure, N-V, even when it has undergone transformation. In addition, the sentence is marked by an intonation pattern which allows the speaker-listener to sense its beginning and end and to feel that in some sense it constitutes a unit. The most common intonation pattern is 2-3-1, and there are a relatively small number of transformed intonation patterns. A formal definition, then, might read like this: *a sentence is a linguistic unit consisting of sound and meaning symbols that follow the structural pattern N-V and produce an intonation pattern satisfactory to the speaker-listener.*

By way of contrast, here is a more traditional definition: "a sentence is a group of words having a subject and a predicate and expressing a complete thought." Besides ignoring the role of intonation, the traditional version presents us with a phrase—"a complete thought"—which is nearly impossible to interpret.

Whatever formal definition we choose, we are now ready to develop some additional procedures of sentence formation. Our previous grammars, though effective, cannot by themselves account for sentences as seemingly simple as *The little girl ran away,* or for sentences like *I know who won the prize* and *The boy who won the prize is an excellent performer.* All these examples derive from double bases—that is, from combinations of more than one kernel sentence.

78

Double-Base Transformations

The seemingly uncomplicated sentence *The little girl ran away* cannot be derived by the PS rules and single-base transformations of Gt Grammar I or II, because neither of these grammars provides a rewrite rule incorporating an adjectival form in the NP segment. *The little girl ran away* actually derives from two deep structures: *The girl ran away* and *The girl is little.* Combining the two deep structures involves two transformations, the *relative* transformation and a transformation that places the adjective before the noun.

THE RELATIVE TRANSFORMATION (T-rel)
AND THE ADJECTIVE + NOUN
TRANSFORMATION (T-adj + N)

To begin the derivation of *The little girl ran away,* we can combine the two deep structures in the following order:

The girl — the girl is little — ran away.

To state that speakers never use such a construction is too absolute. In times of stress, they may do so; but usually they avoid the redundant *The girl, the girl.* One way to avoid it is to replace the second NP with a relative pronoun such as *who.* The resulting structure—*who is little*—is termed a *relative clause,* derived by the T-rel. A string progression shows the two deep-structure kernel strings and the necessary transformations:

Deep structures: the + girl + sing. + past + run + away
                   the + girl + sing. + pres. + be + little

    T-rel ⇒   the + girl + sing. + who + pres. + be +
              little + past + run + away

    T-af ⇒   the + girl + sing. + who + be + pres. +
              little + run + past + away
              # the # girl + sing. # who # be + pres.
              # little # run + past # away #

At this point, a morphographemic string would indicate that the resulting sentence is *The girl who is little ran away.* To create *The little girl ran away* we must add two more transformations preceding the T-af:

Deep structures: the + girl + sing. + past + run + away
                    the + girl + sing. + pres. + be + little
    T-rel ⇒   the + girl + sing. + who + pres. + be +
                    little + past + run + away
    T-del ⇒   the + girl + sing. + little + past + run +
                    away
T-adj + N ⇒   the + little + girl + sing. + past + run +
                    away
    T-af ⇒   the + little + girl + sing. + run + past +
                    away
                    # the # little # girl + sing. # run + past
                    # away #
                    The little girl ran away.

Essentially the same procedure creates what is traditionally termed an *appositive,* which may be illustrated by the following progression:

Deep structures: John + past + do + the + work + sing.
                    John + pres. + be + a + plumber + sing.
    T-rel ⇒   John + who + pres. + be + a + plumber
                    + sing. + past + do + the + work +
                    sing.
    T-del ⇒   John + a + plumber + sing. + past + do
                    + the + work + sing.
    T-af ⇒   John + a + plumber + sing. + do + past
                    + the + work + sing.
                    # John # a # plumber + sing. # do +
                    past # the # work + sing. #
                    John, a plumber, did the work.

In this case, we could label the T-del string *T-appositive* and write the rule that deletes the relative pronoun and the tense and *be* structure.

T-rel leads us to note several additional characteristics of the sentence-forming act. One is the necessity, which we have remarked before, of ordering the transformations correctly; for instance, in the progression for *The little girl ran away,* the order must be T-rel, T-del, T-adj + N. Another characteristic is the part that lexical entries may have in the choice of a relative pronoun: since *girl* is +human, the +human pronoun *who* is used rather than the −human pronoun *which.*

A third characteristic is generally termed *recursiveness* or *recursion*.

Recursion permits the infinite repetition of linguistic units:

> I saw the girl *who saw her friend who was with a friend who was a newcomer who had recently moved to town.*

Recursion is a characteristic of many sentences that derive from more than one deep structure. Even if it is not apparent in the morphographemic string, it may have occurred at some point during the sentence's derivation: for example, *The pretty little girl ran away* may at one stage have been *The girl who is pretty who is little ran away.* We say "may" because there will often be disagreement in analyzing such abstract entities as deep structures, particularly those in a recursive sentence.

Despite possible disagreement, the reader will profit from attempting to work out the deep structures in the following sentences formed by T-rel.

1. I saw a huge alligator which was floating in a stagnant pond.
2. The alligator which I saw ate a frog which was green.
3. Alligators which live in small ponds provide an ecological balance.
4. *Ecology* is a term which is used by conservationists.

T-rel is only one way by which speakers accumulate sentence units to achieve economy and tighter "meaning." Other ways are discussed in the following sections.

THE NOUN CLAUSE TRANSFORMATION (T-N-cl)

T-N-cl may be distinguished from T-rel at its deep-structure level. In a sentence such as *I know who you are* a noun clause has been substituted for the indefinite "something":

Deep structures: I + pres. + know + "something"
                  You + pres. + be + "someone"
  T-N-cl ⇒ I + pres. + know + who + you + pres. + be
  T-af ⇒ I + know + pres. + who + you + be + pres.

I # know + pres. # who # you # be +
pres. #
I know who you are.

Essentially the same progression will derive *I know that people shoot geese* and *I know what you do*. T-N-cl can also create sentences whose subordinate noun clauses are headed by a word other than a relative pronoun: *I know when you left home, I know where you went*.

Sentences which use *that* to introduce the subordinate noun clause are peculiar in this respect: the *that* can usually be deleted with no obvious change in meaning, as when *I know that people shoot geese* is altered to *I know people shoot geese*. In contrast, if we delete the *when* in *I know when you left home*, we create an entirely different sentence, with a different deep structure.

THE ADVERB CLAUSE TRANSFORMATION (T-adv-cl)

The PS rule for the verbal shows that an adverbial word or prepositional phrase may appear either along with or in place of a predicate N form:

$$\text{verbal} \rightarrow (\text{aux}) + \begin{Bmatrix} Vi \\ Vt \end{Bmatrix} + \begin{Bmatrix} (NP) \\ (adj) \\ (adv) \end{Bmatrix} + (adv)$$

This rule will create such sentences as:

He does the work *frequently*.
He rode the horse *skeptically*.
He went to town *in the morning*.
He placed the cup *on the drainboard*.
He worked on the boat *for money*.

The adverbial form in each of these examples adds a meaning of frequency, manner, time, place, or reason to the rest of the sentence. But instead of using adverbial words or phrases, speakers can create similar meanings by using *adverbial subordinate clauses:*

He does the work *whenever time permits*.
He rode the horse *although he was apprehensive*.
He went to town *when morning came*.

He placed the cup *where he wanted it.*
He worked on the boat *because he earned money.*

Each of these sentences can be derived by a T-adv-cl rule. One of the deep-structure strings signals an appropriate Dc word, as *when* is signaled by "sometime" in the following progression.

Deep structures: He + past + go + to + NULL + town +
                  sing. + "sometime"
                  NULL + morning + sing. + past + come

T-adv-cl ⇒ He + past + go + to + NULL + town +
            sing. + when + NULL + morning +
            sing. + past + come

T-af ⇒ He + go + past + to + NULL + town +
        sing. + when + NULL + morning +
        sing. + come + past
        # He # go + past # to # NULL # town
        + sing. # when # NULL # morning +
        sing. # come + past #
        He went to town when morning came.

THE COORDINATING OR CONJUNCTIVE TRANSFORMATION (T-conj)

It is necessary to distinguish between sentences that join deep structures by transformations like T-rel, T-N-cl, and T-adv-cl, and those that join deep structures by coordination. The latter type of sentence, created by T-conj, contains deep structures that are connected by coordinate Dc forms like *and, or, yet,* and *but,* or by correlative Dc forms like *neither . . . nor.*

The use of T-conj with coordinate Dc forms is obviously quite prevalent. Many speakers tend to connect sentences by a series of *and*'s: *I went to town and I bought a book and I ate dinner and I saw a movie.* Another speaker might say *When I went to town, I bought a book before I ate dinner and after I saw a movie.* The latter sentence derives primarily from T-adv-cl. But the last adverb clause is joined to its similar preceding structure by T-conj.

T-conj is used in combination with T-del and other transformations to create such seemingly uncomplicated sentences as:

> George and Bob walked to town.
> George walked and ran to town.
> George neither walked nor ran to town.
> Neither George nor Bob walked to town.
> I saw George and Bob.
> The job was done by George and Bob.

The last example derives from T-pass and T-conj. A string progression may be written in the following way:

Deep structures:	George + past + do + the + job + sing.
	Bob + past + do + the + job + sing.
T-conj ⇒	George + and + Bob + past + do + the + job + sing.
T-pass ⇒	the + job + sing. + past + be + part. + do + by + George + and + Bob
T-af ⇒	the + job + sing. + be + past + do + part. + by + George + and + Bob
	# the # job + sing. # be + past # do + part. # by # George # and # Bob #

Notice also that T-conj can create what are traditionally termed compound subjects and compound predicates:

Deep structures:	George + past + walk + to + NULL + town + sing.
	Bob + past + walk + to + NULL + town + sing.
T-conj ⇒	George + and + Bob + past + walk + to + NULL + town + sing.
T-af ⇒	George + and + Bob + walk + past + to + NULL + town + sing.
	# George # and # Bob # walk + past # to # NULL # town + sing. #
	George and Bob walked to town.

Deep structures:	George + past + walk + to + NULL + town + sing.
	George + past + run + to + NULL + town + sing.

T-conj ⇒   George + past + walk + and + past + run
+ to + NULL + town + sing.

T-af ⇒   George + walk + past + and + run + past
+ to + NULL + town + sing.

George # walk + past # and # run +
past # to # NULL # town + sing. #
George walked and ran to town.

It is evident that double-base transformations account for
the many ways by which speaker-listeners create and comprehend sentences that derive from more than one deep structure.
We can easily see that generalized sentence labeling—"simple
sentence," "compound sentence," and so forth—may lead to
an inaccurate assessment of the speaker-listener's creative linguistic activity. Though *The little girl ran away* may appear
"simple," it is in fact created by a not-so-simple sequence of
transformations.

A useful supplement to an examination of double-base
transformations is a classification of the different types of *accumulation,* which is another name for the process by which
deep-structure units are combined into multiple-unit sentences.

Accumulation

Our discussion of recursion indicates that linguistic units
like those derived by T-rel, T-adv-cl, T-N-cl, and T-conj may
be infinitely accumulated. Accumulation is not simply a matter of addition: the accumulated units create a variety of distinct patterns. Notice the variations in the following sentences.

He mowed the yard [after he repaired the mower].
[After he repaired the mower] he mowed the yard.
Bill [who is my son] mowed the yard.
The yard was mowed by Bill [who is my son].
I see [that Bill mowed the yard].
I see [that Bill [who is my son] mowed the yard].
Bill [mowing the yard] cut down the tree.
Bill is mowing the yard and [cutting down the tree].

Each of the bracketed units may be derived by T-rel, T-adv-cl, T-N-cl, or T-conj, and each unit may be said to pattern in a distinct way in respect to the other elements in the sentence.

Every one of the bracketed units in these examples derives directly from a particular deep structure that could have formed a separate sentence. And despite the transformations that have occurred, the bracketed units retain significant amounts of their original syntactic structure. Units of this sort are called *sentence units* or SU's. *Bill is mowing the yard and cutting down the tree* therefore contains two SU's. A sentence like *The little girl ran away* is considered a single SU, because the deep structure that accounted for *little* has otherwise vanished in the surface syntax. We will continue to use the symbol S to refer to a full sentence, which may include any number of SU's.

In much the same way that Gt theory demonstrates a base component with finite characteristics that permit an infinite number of sentences, an examination of multiple-SU sentences indicates that the speaker-listener has acquired a finite number of SU accumulation patterns that he transforms and combines in an infinite variety of ways to create complicated sentence structures. At the surface-structure level these accumulation patterns can be expressed as rewrite rules that supplement the rules offered by Gt theory. Analysis of the patterns may yield important information about the development of English prose style or, for that matter, about linguistic choice in general. Assuming that two speakers are responding to the same problem, why does one speaker say, "I know the error and I'm going to correct it," while the other says, "I know what's wrong and I'm going to correct it"? Each hypothetical speaker chose a different SU pattern. To describe the various possible patterns, we can classify accumulation into four types: *simple accumulation, simple infixation, ultimate infixation,* and *reduction.*

SIMPLE ACCUMULATION

SU's derived from T-rel, T-adv-cl, and T-conj may be accumulated in a simple fashion to the preceding SU or SU's:

He went to town *when it was dark.* (by T-adv-cl)
The lawn is being mowed by Bill *who is my son.* (by
    T-rel)
He mowed the lawn, and *he raked the yard.* (by T-conj)

In the rewrite rule for such simple accumulation, each SU is numbered sequentially as it appears in the surface structure, and the Dc symbol is used to note that a conjunction of some sort joins the SU's:

$$S \rightarrow SU_1 \quad Dc \quad SU_2$$

A formula of this sort is called an *S string formula.*

We can also represent simple accumulation by an abbreviated tree diagram:

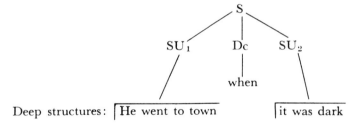

Deep structures:

Since the Dc form is *when,* the derivation is by T-adv-cl. If necessary, the tree can be formally written, using PS rules and string progressions:

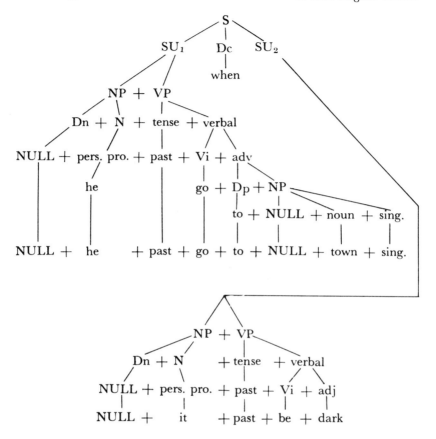

T-adv-cl ⇒ NULL + he + past + go + to + NULL +
              town + sing. + when + NULL + it +
              past + be + dark

A T-af and a morphographemic string then create the sentence *He went to town when it was dark.*

This sort of elaborated tree diagram should not be considered methodology. It is presented here to illustrate the compatibility of S string-formula analysis and Gt theory. A similar relationship could be shown between S string-formula analysis and IC analysis or sentence-pattern designation.

With the introduction of some further symbolism, simple accumulation can account for sentences in which the "regular" order of the SU's has been transformed:

> When it was dark, he went to town.
> $S \rightarrow SU_{1t} \quad || \quad SU_2$
> After it was dark but before it rained, he went to town.
> $S \rightarrow SU_{1t} \quad Dc \quad SU_{2t} \quad || \quad SU_3$
> After it was dark, he went to town when it was raining.
> $S \rightarrow SU_{1t} \quad || \quad SU_2 \quad Dc \quad SU_3$

The subscript t, of course, stands for transformation. In the first of these examples, the "regular" order would have placed *when it was dark* after *he went to town*. We put "regular" in quotes because the regularity is only an abstraction in the mind of the grammarian. The examples also show the use of another symbol, the boundary marked $||$, which denotes an intonational juncture of some duration, a juncture that, in many instances, may replace a Dc form.

Earlier some limitations were placed on the type of structure that can be designated SU. We can now illustrate some additional aspects of these limitations in relation to simple accumulation. A sentence like *Sue and Bill ran down the hill* is *not* an example of accumulation, despite the fact that it obviously derives by T-conj from two deep structures. Because the surface structure does not retain significant syntactic elements from *both* deep structures, the sentence must be considered a single SU. Other examples of this sort of sentence are *I saw Sue and Bill, Sue is sweet and pretty, The lawn was mowed by Bill and Steve.* To put it generally, any two or more noun, adjective, or adverb words joined together by a Dc do *not* evidence multiple SU's. In contrast, a sentence like *Steve mowed the lawn and raked the leaves* does retain significant syntactic elements from both deep structures; it would be analyzed by the simple-accumulation formula

> $S \rightarrow SU_1 \quad Dc \quad SU_2$

and an abbreviated tree would show

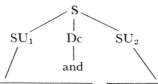

Deep structures: |Steve mowed the lawn |Steve raked the leaves

SIMPLE INFIXATION

Speakers do not always choose to accumulate SU's by the simple means noted in the preceding section. For reasons of syntactic unity, speakers may choose to create sentences such as:

> Bill, who is my son, mowed the yard.
> Sue, when the car wouldn't start, walked to school.
> The small particle, which is called an atom, is powerful.

In sentences like these examples, one SU structure is *infixed* within another. This type of infixation may be called simple infixation because the infixed SU, if removed from the surface structure, leaves the structure of the remaining SU intact. The S string formula for these examples is:

$$S \rightarrow SU_{1a} \quad Dc \quad SU_2 \quad || \quad SU_{1b}$$

By applying the subscripts a and b, the formula notes that SU_2 divides the linguistic elements of SU_1. An abbreviated tree shows the distinction at the deep-structure sentence level:

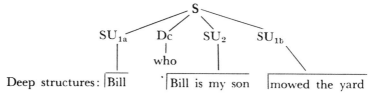

Deep structures: |Bill   '|Bill is my son |mowed the yard

Simple infixation may combine with other accumulations to create an infinite variety of sentences.

It may be useful, as an exercise, to examine the following sentences for simple accumulation and simple infixation. Write the S string formula for each.

    1.   After he saw the accident, the man who was standing nearby called the police.

2. The price of eggs, which has been soaring, reached new heights after the Easter holiday was over.
3. Did you watch the movie that my neighbor, who is a Bogart fan, recommended?
4. When you see my friend, give him the name of the theater that is showing Bogart films.

As another type of exercise, write sentences that can be analyzed according to the following S string formulas.

1. $S \rightarrow SU_{1a}$ Dc SU_2 Dc SU_3 || SU_{1b}
2. $S \rightarrow SU_{1t}$ || SU_{2a} Dc SU_3 || SU_{2b}
3. $S \rightarrow SU_{1t}$ Dc SU_{2t} || SU_3
4. $S \rightarrow SU_{1a}$ Dc SU_2 || SU_{1b} Dc SU_3

ULTIMATE INFIXATION

The sentences that derive by T-N-cl are distinct from those that derive from other clause-forming transformations. T-N-cl creates an infixed SU that cannot be removed from the sentence because it functions as a form-class N that is necessary to the structure of the other SU. For this reason, the term *ultimate infixation* seems proper. And some change in symbolism is needed to distinguish ultimate infixation from simple infixation:

I know who you are.
$S \rightarrow SU_1$ (SU_2)

By enclosing the ultimately infixed SU in parentheses, we note its unique relationship to the other SU. An abbreviated tree may better explain the encompassing aspect of the parentheses:

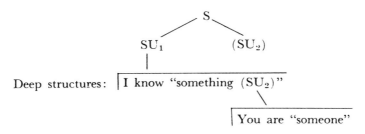

Deep structures:

T-N-cl, T-af, and a morphographemic string can now create
I know who you are.
Ultimate infixation may occur in a variety of ways. Here
are three more examples:

1. *What he wanted* was not attainable.
   S → (SU₁) SU₂
2. She knew *when he did what she wanted.*
   S → SU₁ (SU₂ (SU₃))
3. She agreed with *what he said.*
   S → SU₁ (SU₂)

Abbreviated tree diagrams illustrate the distinct characteristic
of each ultimate infixation:

1.

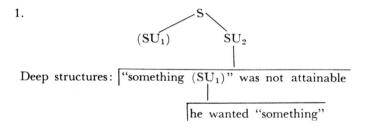

2.

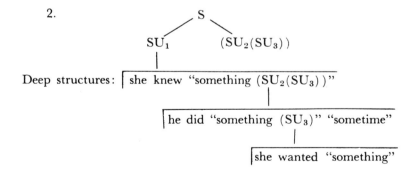

3.

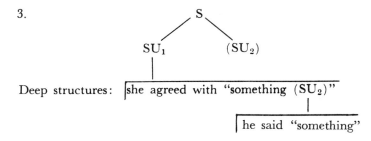

Deep structures: she agreed with "something (SU₂)"

he said "something"

REDUCTION

Simple accumulation, simple infixation, and ultimate infixation are three major accumulation processes. But the speaker-listener also creates and understands sentences in which the forms resulting from each of these processes are *reduced*. The most typical reduced SU is identical with what is traditionally called a "verbal" phrase—that is, a phrase based on a verb, such as an infinitive phrase, a participial phrase, or a gerund phrase. Each of these is derived by deleting certain linguistic elements in a deep structure. Consider the following two sentences from *All the King's Men* by Robert Penn Warren.

Cass found the main door unlocked at the house, entered the hall, saw no one, but heard laughter from above. He mounted the stairs and discovered, at the end of the hall, a small group of men, gathered at an open door.[1]

An S string formula for the first sentence shows simple accumulation:

$$S \rightarrow SU_1 \parallel SU_2 \parallel SU_3 \quad Dc \quad SU_4$$

An S string formula for the second sentence shows both accumulation and reduction:

$$S \rightarrow SU_1 \quad Dc \quad SU_2 \parallel SU_{3R}$$

The addition of the subscript R indicates that, in this example, the final SU—the participial phrase beginning with *gathered*—is a reduction of *who were gathered at an open door,* a clause which itself was derived through T-rel from the deep structure *a small group of men were gathered at an open door.*

Notice the variety of reduced SU structures in the following:

Gathering natural foods was an avocation.
$S \rightarrow (SU_{1R})$ SU_2

Natural foods, *when gathered properly,* last indefinitely.
$S \rightarrow SU_{1a}$ Dc SU_{2R} || SU_{1b}

A desire *to gather natural foods* may prove life-sustaining.
$S \rightarrow SU_{1a}$ || SU_{2R} || SU_{1b}

Steve wanted *to gather natural foods.*
$S \rightarrow SU_1$ (SU_{2R})

Reduction is not confined to "verbal" phrases. In fact, it is a linguistic phenomenon that once again demonstrates the remarkable ability of the speaker-listener to create and comprehend an infinite variety of surface structures with his underlying knowledge of deep structures. Another two sentences from *All the King's Men* illustrate the point:

There he saw the man whom he took to be Mr. Simms, a nondescript fellow in a plug hat, and beyond him the figure of a woman. She was a very young woman, some twenty years old perhaps, rather slender, with skin slightly darker than ivory, probably an octaroon, and hair crisp rather than kinky, and deep dark liquid eyes, slightly bloodshot, which stared at a spot above and beyond the Frenchman.[2]

These two sentences contain some seventeen deep-structure sentences, if we count even the ones whose syntactic structure has disappeared. Most of the seventeen have been reduced, and only one of the resulting phrases would traditionally be called "verbal."

As an exercise, write S string formulas for the following sentences, which have been derived through various combinations of simple accumulation, infixation, and reduction.

1. After leaving the house, Steve drove to the market to buy groceries.
2. The market, which was closed ordinarily, was open all night so that people who worked all day could shop at leisure.
3. The ability to shop at night was a convenience provided by modern marketing methods.
4. Steve drove to another section of town, where a market was open, and bought groceries.

Conclusion

Double-base transformations and S string analysis complete our introduction to linguistic concepts and systems. The study of structural theory, Gt theory, and accumulation should raise questions in the reader's mind, questions about the mental processes involved in linguistic activity and about the social and psychological factors that influence linguistic development and performance. The reader should now have a basis for further reading that will help him to answer those questions. This book is only a beginning.

Notes

1. New York: Harcourt, Brace and World, 1946, p. 190. Copyright 1946 by Robert Penn Warren.
2. *Ibid.*, p. 191.

Suggested Readings

Note: Complete bibliographic information for each entry appears in Appendix C: Selected Bibliography.
Chomsky, Noam, *Aspects of the Theory of Syntax*, 1965, "Aspects of Deep Structure," pp. 65–106. Also in *Chomsky: Selected Readings,* ed. J. P. B. Allen and Paul Van Buren, 1971, pp. 55–68.
————, *Syntactic Structures*, 1957, Chapter 8, "The Explanatory Power of Linguistic Theory," pp. 85–91.
Harris, Zellig S., "Discourse Analysis," *Language*, 28 (1952), 1–30. Also in *The Structure of Language: Readings in the Philosophy of Language,* ed. Jerry A. Fodor and Jerrold J. Katz, 1964, pp. 355–383.
Hughes, John P., *The Science of Language*, 1962, Chapter 9, "Complex Syntactic Structures," pp. 183–193.

APPENDIX A

Suggested Applications

1. Using S string analysis, investigate the changes evident in English prose style from the sixteenth century to the present time. The excerpts that follow are chronologically arranged and, though fragmentary, provide the samples needed to begin the investigation. Some of the questions that may be pursued are: What are the kinds of accumulation? What are their frequencies? How many SU structures are there within the punctuated sentence unit? What conclusions can be drawn about the writer's purpose, the writer's style, and the overall evolution of English prose style?

ROGER ASCHAM, from *The Schoolmaster* (c. 1522)*

There is a way, touched in the first book of Cicero *De oratore,* which, wisely brought into schools, truly taught, and constantly used, would not only take wholly away this butcherly fear in making of Latins but would also, with ease and pleasure and in short time, as I know by good experience, work a true choice and placing of words, a right ordering of sentences, an easy understanding of the tongue, a readiness to speak, a facility to write, a true judgment both of his own and other men's doings, what tongue soever he doth use.

The way is this. After the three concordances learned, as I touched before, let the master read unto him the epistles of Cicero gathered together and chosen out by Sturmius for the capacity of children.

First let him teach the child, cheerfully and plainly, the cause and

---

* Lawrence Ryan, ed. (Ithaca, N.Y.: Cornell University Press, 1967), Book I, pp. 14–15.

matter of the letter; then, let him construe it into English so oft as
the child may easily carry away the understanding of it; lastly, parse
it over perfectly. This done thus, let the child, by and by, both construe and parse it over again so that it may appear that the child
doubteth in nothing that his master taught him before. After this,
the child must take a paper book and, sitting in some place where
no man shall prompt him, by himself, let him translate into English
his former lesson. Then, showing it to his master, let the master
take from him his Latin book, and, pausing an hour at the least,
then let the child translate his own English into Latin again in
another paper book. When the child bringeth it turned into Latin,
the master must compare it with Tully's book and lay them both
together, and where the child doth well, either in choosing or true
placing of Tully's words, let the master praise him and say, "Here ye
do well." For I assure you, there is no such whetstone to sharpen a
good wit and encourage a will to learning as is praise.

JOHN MILTON, from "Of Reformation" (1641)*

From hence then I passe to Qu. ELIZABETH, the next *Protestant*
Prince, in whose Dayes why *Religion* attain'd not a perfect reduce-
ment in the beginning of her Reigne, I suppose the hindring Causes
will be found to bee common with some formerly alledg'd for King
EDWARD 6. the greennesse of the Times, the weake Estate which Qu.
MARY left the Realme in, the great Places and Offices executed by
Papists, the *Judges*, the *Lawyers*, the *Justices* of Peace for the most
part *Popish*, the *Bishops* firme to *Rome*, from whence was to be expected the furious flashing of Excommunications, and absolving the
People from their Obedience. Next, her private *Councellours*, who-
ever they were, perswaded her (as *Camden* writes) that the altering
of *Ecclesiasticall Policie* would move sedition. Then was the *Liturgie*
given to a number of moderate *Divines*, and Sir *Tho. Smith* a States-
man to bee purg'd, and Physick't: And surely they were moderate
Divines indeed, neither hot nor cold; and *Grindall* the best of them,
afterwards *Arch-Bishop* of *Canterbury* lost favour in the Court, and
I think was discharg'd the government of his *See* for favouring the
Ministers, though *Camden* seeme willing to finde another Cause:
therefore about her second Yeare in a *Parliament* of Men and
Minds some scarce well grounded, others belching the soure Crudi-
ties of yesterdayes *Poperie*, those Constitutions of EDW. 6. which as
you heard before, no way satisfi'd the men that made them, are now
establish't for best, and not to be mended. From that time follow'd
nothing but Imprisonments, troubles, disgraces on all those that

* *Complete Prose Works of John Milton* (New Haven: Yale University
Press, 1953), Vol. I, pp. 538–541.

found fault with the *Decrees* of the Convocation, and strait were they branded with the Name of *Puritans*. As for the Queene her selfe, shee was made beleeve that by putting downe *Bishops* her *Prerogative* would be infring'd, of which shall be spoken anon, as the course of Method brings it in. And why the *Prelats* labour'd it should be so thought, ask not them, but ask their Bellies. They had found a good Tabernacle, they sate under a spreading Vine, their Lot was fallen in a faire Inheritance. And these perhaps were the cheife impeachments of a more sound rectifying the *Church* in the Queens Time.

JONATHAN SWIFT, from "Some Considerations upon the Consequences Hoped and Feared from the Death of the Queen" (1714)*

. . . employment was given to the Earl Rivers, to the great discontent of the Duke of Marlborough, who intended it for the Duke of Northumberland, then colonel of the Oxford Regiment, to which the Earl of Hertford was to succeed. Some time after, the chamberlains's staff was disposed of to the Duke of Shrewsbury, in the absence, and without the privity of the Earl of Godolphin. The Earl of Sunderland's removal followed; and lastly, that of the high treasurer himself, whose office was put into commission, whereof Mr. Harley (made at the same time chancellor of the Exchequer) was one. I need say nothing of other removals, which are well enough known and remembered: let it suffice, that in eight or nine months' time the whole face of the court was altered, and very few friends of the former ministry left in any great stations there.

. . .

But the Queen, who had then a great esteem for the person and abilities of Mr. Harley (and in proportion of the other two, though at that time not equally known to her) was deprived of his service with some regret, and upon that and other motives, well known at court, began to think herself hardly used; and several stories ran about, whether true or false, that Her Majesty was not always treated with that duty she might expect. Meantime the church party were loud in their complaints, surmising from the virulence of several pamphlets, from certain bills projected to be brought into parliament, from endeavours to repeal the sacramental test, from the avowed principles, and free speeches of some persons in power, and other jealousies needless to repeat, that ill designs were forming against the religion established.

* *The Prose Works of Jonathan Swift* (London: George Bell, 1901), Vol. V, pp. 422–423.

These fears were all confirmed by the trial of Dr. Sacheverell, which drew the populace as one man into the party against the ministry and parliament.

The ministry were very suspicious that the Queen had still a reserve of favour for Mr. Harley, which appeared by a passage that happened some days after his removal. For the Earl of Godolphin's coach and his, happening to meet near Kensington, the earl a few hours after reproached the Queen that she privately admitted Mr. Harley, and was not without some difficulty undeceived by Her Majesty's asseverations to the contrary.

Soon after the doctor's trial, this gentleman by the Queen's command, and the intervention of Mrs. Masham, was brought up the back stairs; and that princess, spirited by the addresses from all parts, which shewed the inclinations of her subjects to be very averse from the proceedings in court and parliament; was resolved to break the united power of the Marlborough and Godolphin families, and to begin this work, by taking the disposal of employments into her own hands; for which an opportunity happened by the death of the Earl of Essex, Lieutenant of the Tower. . . .

T. BABINGTON MACAULAY, from "Frederic the Great" (1842)*

Early in the year 1740, Frederic William met death with a firmness and dignity worthy of a better and wiser man; and Frederic, who had just completed his twenty-eighth year, became King of Prussia. His character was little understood. That he had good abilities, indeed, no person who had talked with him or corresponded with him could doubt. But the easy Epicurean life which he had led, his love of good cookery and good wine, of music, of conversation, of light literature, led many to regard him as a sensual and intellectual voluptuary. His habit of canting about moderation, peace, liberty, and the happiness which a good mind derives from the happiness of others had imposed on some who should have known better. Those who thought best of him expected a Telemachus after Fénelon's pattern. Others predicted the approach of a Medicean age—an age propitious to learning and art, and not unpropitious to pleasure. Nobody had the least suspicion that a tyrant of extraordinary military and political talents, of industry more extraordinary still, without fear, without faith, and without mercy, had ascended the throne.

The disappointment of Falstaff at his old boon-companion's coronation was not more bitter than that which awaited some of the

* *Miscellaneous Works of Lord Macaulay* (New York: Harper Brothers, n.d.), Vol. III, pp. 280–281.

inmates of Rheinsberg. They had long looked forward to the accession of their patron as to the event from which their own prosperity and greatness were to date. They had at last reached the promised land—the land which they had figured to themselves as flowing with milk and honey—and they found it a desert. "No more of these fooleries," was the short, sharp admonition given by Frederic to one of them. It soon became plain that, in the most important points, the new sovereign bore a strong family likeness to his predecessor. There was, indeed, a wide difference between the father and the son as respected extent and vigor of intellect, speculative opinions, amusements, studies, outward demeanor. But the groundwork of the character was the same in both. To both were common the love of order, the love of business, the military taste, the parsimony, the imperious spirit, the temper irritable even to ferocity, the pleasure in the pain and humiliation of others. . . .

CHRISTOPHER MORLEY, from "Frank Confessions of a Publisher's Reader" (1916)*

Great men have graced the job—and got out of it as soon as possible. George Meredith was a reader once; so was Frank Norris; also E. V. Lucas and Gilbert Chesterton. One of the latter's comments on a manuscript is still preserved. Writing of a novel by a lady who was the author of many unpublished stories, all marked by perseverance rather than talent, he said, "Age cannot wither nor custom stale her infinite lack of variety." But alas, we hear too little of these gentlemen in their capacity as publishers' pursuivants. Patrolling the porches of literature, why did they not bequeath us some pandect of their experience, some rich garniture of commentary on the adventures that befell? But they, and younger men such as Coningsby Dawson and Sinclair Lewis, have gone on into the sunny hayfields of popular authorship and said nothing.

But these brilliant swallow-tailed migrants are not typical. Your true specimen of manuscript reader is the faithful old percheron who is content to go on, year after year, sorting over the literary pemmican that comes before him, inexhaustible in his love for the delicacies of good writing, happy if once or twice a twelve-month he chance upon some winged thing. He is not the pettifogging pilgarlic of popular conception: he is a devoted servant of letters, willing to take his thirty or forty dollars a week, willing to suffer the *peine forte et dure* of his profession in the knowledge of honest duty done, writing terse and marrowy little essays on manuscripts, which are buried in the publishers' files. This man is an honour to the profession, and I believe there are many such. Certainly there

* *Essays* (Garden City, N.Y.: Doubleday, Doran, 1928), pp. 84–85.

are many who sigh wistfully when they must lay aside some cherished writing of their own to devote an evening to illiterate twaddle. Five book manuscripts a day, thirty a week, close to fifteen hundred a year—that is a fair showing for the head reader of a large publishing house.

JAMES THURBER, from "Ivorytown, Rinsoville, Anacinburg, and Crisco Corners" (1948)*

The people of Soapland are subject to a set of special ills. Temporary blindness, preceded by dizzy spells and headaches, is a common affliction of Soapland people. The condition usually clears up in six or eight weeks, but once in a while it develops into brain tumor and the patient dies. One script writer, apparently forgetting that General Mills was the sponsor of his serial, had one of his women characters go temporarily blind because of an allergy to chocolate cake. There was hell to pay, and the writer had to make the doctor in charge of the patient hastily change his diagnosis. Amnesia strikes almost as often in Soapland as the common cold in our world. There have been as many as eight or nine amnesia cases on the air at one time. The hero of "Rosemary" stumbled around in a daze for months last year. When he regained his memory, he found that in his wanderings he had been lucky enough to marry a true-blue sweetie. The third major disease is paralysis of the legs. This scourge usually attacks the good males. Like mysterious blindness, loss of the use of the legs may be either temporary or permanent. The hero of "Life Can Be Beautiful" was confined to a wheel chair until his death last March, but young Dr. Malone, who was stricken with paralysis a year ago, is up and around again. I came upon only one crippled villain in 1947: Spencer Hart rolled through a three-month sequence of "Just Plain Bill" in a wheel chair. When their men are stricken, the good women become nobler than ever. A disabled hero is likely to lament his fate and indulge in self-pity now and then, but his wife or sweetheart never complains. She is capable of twice as much work, sacrifice, fortitude, endurance, ingenuity, and love as before. Joyce Jordan, M.D., had no interest in a certain male until he lost the use of both legs and took to a wheel chair. Then love began to bloom in her heart. The man in the wheel chair has come to be the standard Soapland symbol of the American male's subordination to the female and his dependence on her greater strength of heart and soul.

The children of the soap towns are subject to pneumonia and strange fevers, during which their temperatures run to 105 or 106.

* *The Beast in Me and Other Animals* (New York: Hearst, 1948), pp. 170–171.

Several youngsters are killed every year in automobile accidents or die of mysterious illnesses. Infantile paralysis and cancer are never mentioned in serials, but Starr, the fretful and errant wife in "Ma Perkins," died of tuberculosis in March as punishment for her sins. There are a number of Soapland ailments that are never named or are vaguely identified by the doctors as "island fever" or "mountain rash." A variety of special maladies affect the glands in curious ways. At least three Ivorytown and Rinsoville doctors are baffled for several months every year by strange seizures and unique symptoms.

2. Using any of the preceding excerpts (or any segment of English prose), investigate the kinds and scope of transformations. Again, relate your findings to purpose and style.

3. Select one of William Shakespeare's sonnets. Using both S string analysis and an analysis of transformations, draw some conclusions about the form of the Shakespearean sonnet and the relationship between syntactic parallelism and meter. Then contrast Shakespeare's sonnet form with some other sonnet forms.

4. Select some passages from Walt Whitman's *Leaves of Grass* and analyze his free verse form, using S string analysis.

5. Fiction writers create situations by a variety of prose techniques. Choose excerpts from two quite different pieces of fiction—from Henry James' "The Real Thing" and Ernest Hemingway's "A Clean, Well-Lighted Place," for example—and contrast the two authors' uses of immediate and transferred utterance.

6. Many nonfiction prose anthologies arrange their selections according to rhetorical type. Using both S string analysis and an analysis of transformations, draw some conclusions about the relationship between rhetorical modes and structure.

APPENDIX B

Answers to Exercises

1. his | book | wa | s | ly | ing | on | the | table

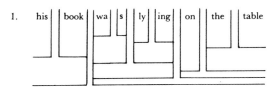

2. the | table | s | beside | the | desk | we | re | large

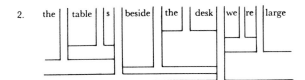

3. library | table | s | a | re | buil | t | sturdi | ly

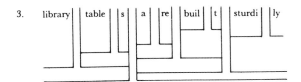

4. many | librarie | s | ha | ve | reading | room | s

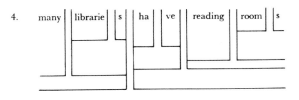

5.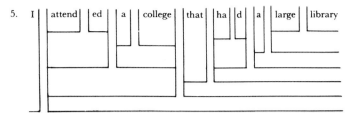

6.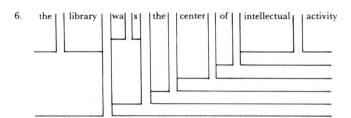

7.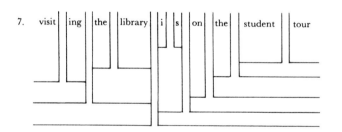

8.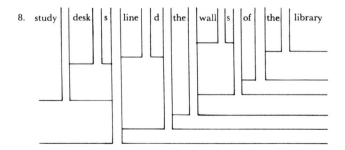

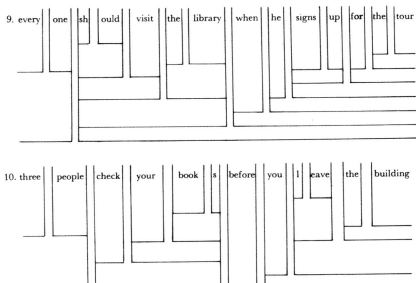

9. every | one | sh | ould | visit | the | library | when | he | signs | up | for | the | tour

10. three | people | check | your | book | s | before | you | l | eave | the | building

PAGE 43

1. The base pattern is N-V-adv. The structure *six miles* may commute with *far* or other adv forms.

2. The base pattern is N-V-adv. The deep structures might be *the clown is silly* (N-V-adj) and *the clown emerged from the tent* (N-V-adv).

3. The deep-structure base patterns are N-V-adj and N-V-adj. *Performance* may take a plural bound morpheme.

4. The bound morpheme *ly* and the fact that *hastilièr* is not acceptable indicate that the word is an adverb.

5. *Traveling* was in the V form class in the deep structure *the man was traveling*.

6. *With red hair* is adjectival. Possible deep structures would include *the boy has hair* and *the hair is red*.

7. The positions of *queen* and *the beautiful woman* may be reversed without much change in meaning.

8. *Who* is both a subordinative Dc and the N for the N-V structure *who broke*. The deep structures are *he is the boy* and *the boy broke the window*.

9. The unit *who saw you* is an N. The pronoun is in the nominative case because it itself is the N in the structure *who saw*.

10. *His* is marked with two symbols because it is both a pronoun and a signaler of the possessive. The Di + V structure is called an infinitive.

PAGES 43-44

   N   V Di V   Dn N   ⌐Dc⌐ NEG adv
1. Rolf proceeds to describe the ways in which not only

  adj   Dc adj   N   adj Dc adj   N
emotional but physical trauma, childhood or sports accidents,

 N V adv V Dn ⌐N⌐ Dn N   ⌐V⌐
etc., can also upset the body-balance. Such accidents lead to

Dn N < adj   N   DcN ⌐V⌐ N Dp
a series of bodily compensations, which may give rise to

 adj   N   Dc N Dc Dn N < N
physical limitations and distortions and a feeling of weakness

Dc N   Dp Dn N DcN V adv   V   Dp adj
or instability in the body which is then transmitted to mental

Dc adj   N
or emotional states.

Comments: In which, a phrase that can commute with *by which, through which*, and so forth, forms a two-word subordinative conjunction. *Body-balance* when hyphenated becomes a single N form, *Lead to* is a V form containing the particle *to*.

   Dp   ⌐ N   adv Dn N   Dp Dn
2. Along Constitution Avenue, just one block from the

     ⌐N⌐   Dp N   V Dn adj   adj
Department of Justice in Washington, stands a granite pillared

  N V Dn   ⌐N⌐   V   adv Dp
building called the National Archives. Enshrined there, under

 N Dp N Di V V N>   N   Dc   ⌐N
glass, for all to see, are our Constitution and Declaration of

N⌐   Dn V N Dn N
Independence. Thousands view them each week.

```
Dp Dn  adj   N  <  Dn   N   Dn   N  < Dn  N    V
```
On the other side of the world, the body of a man named

```
N     V     V      Dp    N  Dp Dn  N   Dp   N     Dc
```
Lenin lies preserved under glass in a tomb in Moscow, and

```
Dn      ——V——   Dn   N    adv
```
thousands pass through that shrine also.

```
Dp   N    Dc  N  V     N      ——N——     V    adv
```
In 1955, when I visited Moscow, Joseph Stalin was there

```
Dp   N    Dp   N    Dc  adv   N    ——V——
```
under glass with Lenin. But now Stalin has been removed.

Comments: Preserved is a V form that heads an endocentric structure that functions as a form-class unit. *Thousands* is properly a Dn but may be considered an N in its use here; the base structure is obviously *thousands of people,* the *of people* having been deleted. *Pass through* is V + particle.

```
      adj    N   Dp    N    V  Di V   Dp  Dn   N    Dc
```
3. Another system in language has to do with the sounds that

```
N    V   Dc   N    V   N  ——V——   Dp    N    Dp
```
we use when we speak. It is known among linguists as

```
  N       N     adv   ——V——   Dn   N  <  Dn
```
"phonology." We commonly think of the sounds of the

```
N    —Dp—  Dn   N      N     Dc   N   Dc   adv
```
language as of two kinds, consonants and vowels. But there

```
V   adv   N   <   N   Dc    N     N  Dn    adv
```
are also features of stress and intonation. All these together

```
V    Dn    N     Dn    N   ——V——  Dp   Dn
```
constitute the phonology. The units are known to many

```
N    Dp    N
```
linguists as "phonemes."

Comments: As and *as of* are used as Dp's in the sense of *in the character of. These* is a Dn that in this case functions as an N, substituting for the full phrase *of these features.*

```
     Dc  adv Dn  adj    N      V        N    ——V—— Dn  N
```
4. But as the new century dawned, Garland turned to a world

```
 <    adj   N    V  Dp Dn   ——N——  <  Dn  ——N
```
of romantic escapism, set in the High Country of the Rocky

```
N——        Dc   V   Dp   N     N     adj    N
```
Mountains, and dealing with cowboys, Indians, forest rangers,

Dc   adj   N   Dn   N   <   Dn   N   V   adv Dn
and cattle barons. The bulk of this work showed only a

adj   N   Dp adj   N   Dc   V   adj   adj   N
residual interest in social themes, and had little artistic merit.

N>   ⌒V⌒   N   Dp adv adj   N   <   V
His turn to romanticism after so many years of preaching

N   V   adj   Dc   adj   N   V   adj   N
realism was startling but logical. He approached middle age

Dp   adj   Di   V   Dp N>   N   N   V   Dn N   Dc
with little to show for his sacrifices. He acquired a wife and

N   Di   V   N   V   Dn   adj   N
family to support. He loved the adventuresome outdoors

⌒adv⌒   Dc   N   V   Dn   adj   adj   N   Dp   N   Dp
so much that he joined the Alaska gold rush in 1898 without

Dn   adj   N   V   Dp Dn   N   <   adj   N
a second thought. Disappointed at the passing of social issues

N ⌒⌒⌒V⌒⌒⌒ Dn adv   adj   Dc N>   N   ⌒⌒⌒V⌒⌒⌒
he had fought for, a trifle bitter that his work had accomplished

adv adj   Dp   N   N   V   adv   Dp Dn   adj   N
so little for reform, he turned frankly for a backward look,

V   Dp   N   Dn   N   Dc   N   <   N   N   V
seeking in nostalgia the comfort and sense of purpose he could

NEG   V   Dp   N   Dc   N
not attain in reform or Realism.

Comments: As commutes with *when. Dealing, preaching,* and
seeking are V forms derived from their own deep structures;
the endocentric structures they form function as form classes.
Turn to is a variant form of *turning to,* a V + particle. *Little*
in the phrases *with little to show for his sacrifices* and *so little
for reform* is an adj that has an IC relationship with an
ambiguous "something."

PAGES 60–61

1. Quite a few sentences can be derived from the rewrite rules
listed; here are three examples:

   The animal could be running from the house.
   These animals should be running rapidly.
   The animal should be being angry.

The tree, T-af string, and morphographemic string for the
third example are as follows:

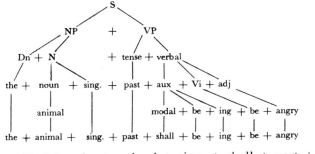

T-af ⇒   the + animal + sing. + shall + past + be
         + be + ing + angry
         # the # animal + sing. # shall + past #
         be # be + ing # angry #

2. a)

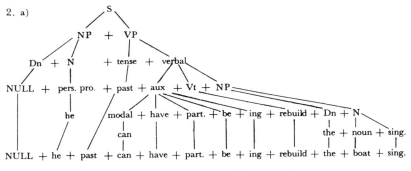

T-af ⇒   he + can + past + have + be + part. +
         rebuild + ing + the + boat + sing.
         # he # can + past # have # be + part.
         # rebuild + ing # the # boat + sing. #

b)

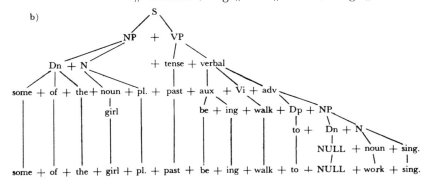

T-af ⇒   some + of + the + girl + pl. + be + past
+ walk + ing + to + NULL + work +
sing.
some # of # the # girl + pl. # be +
past # walk + ing # to # NULL #
work + sing. #

c)

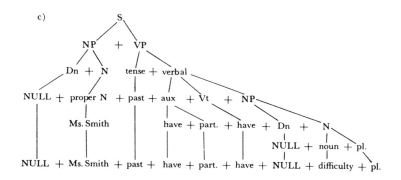

T-af ⇒   NULL + Ms. Smith + have + past + have
+ part. + NULL + difficulty + pl.
# NULL # Ms. Smith # have + past #
have + part. # NULL # difficulty +
pl. #

d)

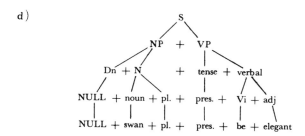

T-af ⇒   NULL + swan + pl. + be + pres. + elegant
NULL # swan + pl. # be + pres.
elegant #

e)

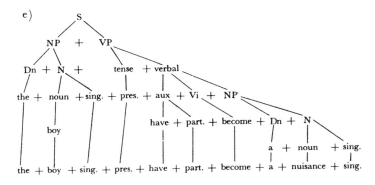

$$T\text{-af} \Rightarrow \text{the + boy + sing. + have + pres. + become + part. + a + nuisance + sing.}$$
$$\text{# the # boy + sing. # have + pres. # become + part. # a # nuisance + sing. #}$$

PAGE   68

1.

the + hunter + sing. + past + find + the + goose + pl.

T-do ⇒ the + hunter + sing. + past + do + find + the + goose + pl.

T-neg ⇒ the + hunter + sing. + past + do + n't + find + the + goose + pl.

T-af ⇒ the + hunter + sing. + do + past + n't + find + the + goose + pl.

the # hunter + sing. # do + past + n't # find # the # goose + pl.

2.

he + past + look + for + the + goose + pl. + "somewhere"

T-q ⇒ past + he + look + for + the + goose + pl. + "somewhere"

T-do ⇒ past + do + he + look + for + the + goose + pl. + "somewhere"

Tq-wh ⇒ where + past + do + he + look + for + the + goose + pl.

T-af ⇒ where + do + past + he + look + for + the + goose + pl.

where # do + past # he # look # for
the # goose + pl.

3.   NULL + hunter + pl. + pres. + have +
                        part. + see + NULL + goose + pl.
T-pass ⇒   NULL + goose + pl. + pres. + have +
                        part. + be + part. + see + by + NULL
                        + hunter + pl.
T-q ⇒   pres. + have + NULL + goose + pl. +
                        part. + be + part. + see + by + NULL
                        + hunter + pl.
T-af ⇒   have + pres. + NULL + goose + pl. + be
                        + part. + see + part. + by + NULL +
                        hunter + pl.
                        # have + pres. # NULL # goose + pl. #
                        be + part. # see + part. # by # NULL
                        # hunter + pl. #

4.   people + pres. + shoot + NULL + goose
                        + pl. + "for some reason"
T-q ⇒   pres. + people + shoot + NULL + goose
                        + pl. + "for some reason"
T-do ⇒   pres. + do + people + shoot + NULL +
                        goose + pl. + "for some reason"
Tq-wh ⇒   why + pres. + do + people + shoot +
                        NULL + goose + pl.
T-af ⇒   why + do + pres. + people + shoot +
                        NULL + goose + pl.
                        # why # do + pres. # people # shoot
                        # NULL # goose + pl. #

5.   you + pres. + be + ing + go + to + the
                        + country + "sometime"
T-q ⇒   pres. + be + you + ing + go + to + the
                        + country + "sometime"
Tq-wh ⇒   when + pres. + be + you + ing + go +
                        to + the + country
T-af ⇒   when + be + pres. + you + go + ing + to
                        + the + country
                        # when # be + pres. # you # go + ing
                        # to # the # country #

PAGE 70

1. T-reflex; T-adv; T-del; T-af
2. T-reflex; T-q; T-do; Tq-wh; T-af
3. T-reflex; T-adv; T-del; T-q; T-do; T-af
4. T-reflex; T-pass; T-neg; T-af
5. T-reflex; T-adv; T-del; T-q; Tq-wh; T-af

PAGE 81

1. I saw an alligator.
   The alligator was huge.
   The alligator was floating in a pond.
   The pond was stagnant.
2. The alligator ate a frog.
   I saw the alligator.
   The frog was green.
3. Alligators provide a balance.
   The balance is ecological.
   Alligators live in ponds.
   The ponds are small.
4. *Ecology* is a term.
   Conservationists use the term.

PAGES 90–91

1. SU_{1t} || SU_{2a} Dc SU_3 || SU_{2b}
2. SU_{1a} Dc SU_2 || SU_{1b} Dc SU_3
3. SU_1 Dc SU_{2a} Dc SU_3 || SU_{2b}
4. SU_{1t} || SU_2 Dc SU_3

Many sentences can be created for each S string formula. A sample for each appears below:

1. The truce which was signed after the city fell was broken many times.
2. When the truce was signed, the army that held the city did not surrender its guns.
3. Before the battle was over and before the city fell, the citizens fled.
4. The citizens, who had endured many hardships, were terrorized by the troops because they fled.

PAGE 94

1. SU_{1t} ‖ SU_2 ‖ SU_{3R}
2. SU_{1a} Dc SU_2 ‖ SU_{1b} Dc SU_{3a} Dc SU_4 ‖ SU_{3b}
3. SU_{1a} ‖ SU_{2R} ‖ SU_{1b} ‖ SU_{3R}
4. SU_1 Dc SU_2 Dc SU_3

APPENDIX C

Selected Bibliography

The entries in this bibliography are intended to provide a useful guide to further study not only in the areas emphasized in this book but also in other important aspects of linguistics. Note that the entries which appeared as "Suggested Readings" appended to each of the first four chapters are marked with asterisks: you should investigate these sources first. The other entries, besides dealing with phonology, morphology, and syntax, provide references for beginning investigations in tagmemics, social dialectology, kinesics, proxemics, and psycholinguistics; some of the works demonstrate applications of linguistic theory to the teaching of reading and to the study of literature.

Allen, Harold B., Bibliography in *Linguistics and English Linguistics*, New York: Appleton-Century-Crofts, 1966.
————, *Readings in Applied Linguistics*, New York: Appleton-Century-Crofts, 1958.
*Allen, J. P. B., and Paul Van Buren, eds., *Chomsky: Selected Readings*, London: Oxford University Press, 1971.
Alston, William P., *Philosophy of Language*, Englewood Cliffs, N.J.: Prentice-Hall, 1964.
Bach, Emmon, *An Introduction to Transformational Grammars*, New York: Holt, Rinehart and Winston, 1964.
————, and Robert T. Harms, eds., *Universals in Linguistic Theory*, New York: Holt, Rinehart and Winston, 1968.
Baugh, Albert C., *A History of the English Language*, New York: Appleton-Century-Crofts, 1957, 1963.
Benjamin, Robert L., *Semantics and Language Analysis*, New York: Bobbs-Merrill, 1970.

Birdwhistle, Ray L., *Introduction to Kinesics*, Louisville, Ky.: University of Louisville Press, 1952.
——, *Kinesics and Context*, Philadelphia: University of Pennsylvania Press, 1970.
*Bloomfield, Leonard, *Language*, New York: Holt, Rinehart and Winston, 1933, 1961.
Bloomfield, Morton W., and Leonard Newmark, *A Linguistic Introduction to the English Language*, New York: Knopf, 1964.
*Bolinger, Dwight, *Aspects of Language*, New York: Harcourt, Brace and World, 1968.
Botha, Rudolf P., *The Methodological Status of Grammatical Argumentation*, The Hague: Mouton, 1970.
Brook, G. L., *English Dialects*, London: André Deutsch, 1963.
Brown, Huntington, *Prose Styles*, Minneapolis: University of Minnesota Press, 1966.
Carroll, John B., *Language and Thought*, Englewood Cliffs, N.J.: Prentice-Hall, 1964.
——, *Language, Thought and Reality: Selected Writings of Benjamin Lee Whorf*, Cambridge, Mass.: M.I.T. Press, 1956.
*Chafe, Wallace L., *Meaning and the Structure of Language*, Chicago: University of Chicago Press, 1970.
*Chomsky, Noam, *Aspects of the Theory of Syntax*, Cambridge, Mass.: M.I.T. Press, 1965.
*——, *Cartesian Linguistics*, New York: Harper and Row, 1966.
——, *Current Issues in Linguistic Research*, The Hague: Mouton, 1957.
*——, *Language and Mind*, enlarged edition, New York: Harcourt, Brace, Jovanovich, 1972.
*——, *Syntactic Structures*, The Hague: Mouton, 1957.
*——, and Morris Halle, *The Sound Pattern of English*, New York: Harper and Row, 1968.
* Clark, Virginia P., Paul A. Eschholz, and Alfred F. Rosa, eds., *Language: Introductory Readings*, New York: St. Martin's, 1972.
Cook, Walter A., *Introduction to Tagmemic Analysis*, New York: Holt, Rinehart and Winston, 1969.
——, *On Tagmemes and Transforms*, Washington, D.C.: Georgetown University Press, 1964.
Deese, James, *Psycholinguistics*, Boston: Allyn and Bacon, 1970.
*Dinneen, Francis P., *An Introduction to General Linguistics*, New York: Holt, Rinehart and Winston, 1967.
*Fodor, Jerry A., and Jerrold J. Katz, *The Structure of Language: Readings in the Philosophy of Language*, Englewood Cliffs, N.J.: Prentice-Hall, 1964.
Francis, W. Nelson, *The English Language: An Introduction*, New York: Norton, 1963, 1965.

*————, *The Structure of American English,* New York: Ronald Press, 1958.

Fries, Charles Carpenter, *American English Grammar,* New York: Appleton-Century-Crofts, 1940.

————, *Linguistics and Reading,* New York: Holt, Rinehart and Winston, 1963.

*————,*The Structure of English,* New York: Harcourt, Brace, 1952.

Fries, Peter H., "Tagmemics," in *Language: Introductory Readings,* ed. Virginia P. Clark, Paul A. Eschholz, and Alfred F. Rosa, New York: St. Martin's, 1972, pp. 194–208.

*Gleason, H. A., Jr., *An Introduction to Descriptive Linguistics,* revised edition, New York: Holt, Rinehart and Winston, 1961.

*————, *Linguistics and English Grammar,* New York: Holt, Rinehart and Winston, 1965.

*Grady, Michael, *Syntax and Semantics of the English Verb Phrase,* The Hague: Mouton, 1970.

Hall, Edward T., "Proxemics," *Current Anthropology,* 9 (1968), 83–104.

Halle, Morris, "Phonology in Generative Grammar," *Word,* 18 (1962), 54–72. Also in Fodor and Katz, q.v.

Harms, Robert T., *Introduction to Phonological Theory,* Englewood Cliffs, N.J.: Prentice-Hall, 1968.

*Harris, Zellig S., "Discourse Analysis," *Language,* 28 (1952), 1–30. Also in Fodor and Katz, q.v.

————, "Distributional Structure," in *Linguistics Today,* ed. A. Martinet and V. Weinreich, New York: Linguistic Circle of New York, 1954, pp. 26–42.

————, *Structural Linguistics,* Chicago: University of Chicago Press, 1951.

Hill, Archibald A., *Introduction to Linguistic Structures,* New York: Harcourt, Brace and World, 1958.

*Hockett, Charles F., *A Course in Modern Linguistics,* New York: Macmillan, 1958.

————, *A Manual of Phonology,* Baltimore: Waverly, 1955.

Hoenigswald, Henry M., *Language Change and Linguistic Reconstruction,* Chicago: The University of Chicago Press, 1960.

*Hughes, John P., *The Science of Language,* New York: Random House, 1962.

Jacobs, Roderick A., and Peter S. Rosenbaum, *English Transformational Grammar,* Waltham, Mass.: Blaisdell, 1968.

Jespersen, Otto, *Analytic Syntax,* New York: Holt, Rinehart and Winston, 1969.

*Katz, Jerrold J., and Paul M. Postal, *An Integrated Theory of Linguistic Descriptions,* Cambridge, Mass.: M.I.T. Press, 1964.

Koutsoudas, Andreas, *Writing Transformational Grammars*, New York: McGraw-Hill, 1966.

Labov, William, "Phonological Correlates of Social Stratification," *American Anthropologist*, 66, Part 2 (1966), 164–176.

——, "The Social Motivation of a Sound Change," *Word*, 19 (1963), 273–309.

——, *The Social Stratification of English in New York City*, Washington, D.C.: Center for Applied Linguistics, 1966.

——, *The Study of Nonstandard English*, Champaign, Ill.: National Council of Teachers of English, 1970.

Langacker, Ronald W., *Language and Its Structure*, New York: Harcourt, Brace and World, 1968.

Langendoen, D. Terence, *Essentials of English Grammar*, New York: Holt, Rinehart and Winston, 1970.

——, *The Study of Syntax*, New York: Holt, Rinehart and Winston, 1969.

Lefevre, Carl A., *Linguistics and the Teaching of Reading*, New York: McGraw-Hill, 1964.

*Lehmann, Winfred P., *Descriptive Linguistics: An Introduction*, New York: Random House, 1972.

*Lewis, M. M., "The Linguistic Development of Children," *Linguistics at Large*, New York: Viking, 1971. Also in Clark, Eschholz, and Rosa, q.v.

*Lloyd, Donald J., and Harry R. Warfel, *American English in Its Cultural Setting*, New York: Knopf, 1965.

Longacre, Robert E., *Grammar Discovery Procedures*, The Hague: Mouton, 1964.

*McNeill, David, *The Acquisition of Language: The Study of Developmental Psycholinguistics*, New York: Harper and Row, 1970.

Miles, Josephine, *Style and Proportion: The Language of Prose and Poetry*, Boston: Little, Brown, 1967.

Myers, L. M., *The Roots of Modern English*, Boston: Little, Brown, 1966.

Nida, Eugene A., *Morphology: The Descriptive Analysis of Words*, second edition, Ann Arbor: The University of Michigan Press, 1949.

Nist, John, *A Structural History of English*, New York: St. Martin's, 1966.

Pike, Kenneth L., "Language as Particle, Wave and Field," *The Texas Quarterly*, 2 (1959), 37–54.

——, *Language in Relation to a Unified Theory of the Structure of Human Behaviour*, The Hague: Mouton, 1967.

Postal, Paul M., *Aspects of Phonological Theory*, New York: Harper and Row, 1968.

Pyles, Thomas, and John Algeo, *English: An Introduction to Language*, New York: Harcourt, Brace and World, 1970.

Roberts, Paul, *English Syntax,* alternate edition, New York: Harcourt, Brace and World, 1964.

————, *Modern Grammar,* New York: Harcourt, Brace and World, 1968.

————, *Patterns of English,* New York: Harcourt, Brace and World, 1956.

————, *Understanding English,* New York: Harper and Brothers, 1958.

Salus, Peter H., *Linguistics,* New York: Bobbs-Merrill, 1969.

Shuy, Roger W., *Discovering American Dialects,* Champaign, Ill.: National Council of Teachers of English, 1967.

Spencer, John, ed., *Linguistics and Style,* London: Oxford University Press, 1964.

Stageberg, Norman C., *An Introductory English Grammar,* New York: Holt, Rinehart and Winston, 1965.

*Stevens, Martin, "Modes of Utterance," *College Composition and Communication,* May 1963, 65–72.

Strang, Barbara M., *Modern English Structure,* New York: St. Martin's, 1962.

Thomas, Owen, *Transformational Grammar and the Teaching of English,* New York: Holt, Rinehart and Winston, 1965.

*Trager, George L., and Henry Lee Smith, *An Outline of English Structure,* Norman, Okla.: Studies in Linguistics, Occasional Papers, 3, 1951.

Uitti, Karl D., *Linguistics and Literary Theory,* revised edition, Englewood Cliffs, N.J.: Prentice-Hall, 1969.

*Wardhaugh, Ronald, *Introduction to Linguistics,* New York: McGraw-Hill, 1972.

————, *Reading: A Linguistic Perspective,* New York: Harcourt, Brace and World, 1969.

Waterman, John T., *Perspectives in Linguistics,* second edition, Chicago: University of Chicago Press, 1970.

Wilkinson, Andrew, *The Foundations of Language: Talking and Reading in Young Children,* London: Oxford University Press, 1971.

Ziff, Paul, "On Understanding 'Understanding Utterances,'" in *The Structure of Language,* ed. Jerry A. Fodor and Jerrold J. Katz, Englewood Cliffs, N.J.: Prentice-Hall, 1964, pp. 390–399.

————, *Semantic Analysis,* Ithaca, N.Y.: Cornell University Press, 1960.

Index

Accumulation, 85–94; simple, 87–89; types of, 86. *See also* Infixation; Reduction

Adjective + noun transformation, 79–80

Adjectives, 29–30

Adverb clause transformation, 82–83

Adverbial transformation, 68, 70

Adverbs, 30–31

Affix transformation, 55, 56, 57, 73

Allomorphs, 13, 55, 75

Allophones, 8

Appositives, 80

Ascham, Roger, 96

Base patterns, 14, 20, 22, 39, 45, 52; multiple, 33; types of, 22

Bloomfield, Leonard, 12, 32

Chomsky, Noam, 6, 47, 48, 49, 51, 72

Clauses, 13; adverb, 82–83; noun, 81–82

Commutation, 22, 24, 45

Conjunctions, 31, 35–36, 45

Conjunctive transformation, 83–85

Coordinating transformation. *See* Conjunctive transformation

Deep structures, 24, 45, 48, 79, 81, 86, 94

Deletion transformation, 68–69

Determinants, 31–36, 45; negative, 42, 45

Determiner, noun, 31–32, 45

Dialects, 2

Do transformation, 63–64, 66

Double-base transformations, 79–85, 95

Emphasis. *See* Stress

Endocentric structures, 13, 20, 28, 45

Exocentric structures, 13–14; types of, 14. *See also* Base patterns

Form classes, 25–31, 45; adjective, 29–30; adverb, 30–31; noun, 26–28; verb, 28–29

Fries, Charles Carpenter, 14, 15

Function words, 25, 31–36, 45

Generative-transformational (or Gt) grammar, 47–76; creation of, 49–61; implications of, 75–76; morphophonemic rules of, 55–59; phrase-structure rules of, 49–54; semantic components in, 71–75; theory of, 47–48, 76; transformational rules of, 54–55, 61–71

Generative-transformationalism, 5, 17

Grammar, 6–14, 17. *See also* Generative-transformational grammar

Hughes, John P., 15

Immediate-constituent (IC) analysis, 37–40, 45

Immediate constituents, 21–25, 37, 44

Infinitives, 34